2.50

Contemporary

British and North American Verse

an introductory anthology edited by Martin Booth

Oxford University Press, Walton Street, Oxford OX2 6DP

London Glasgow New York Toronto
Delhi Bombay Calcutta Madras Karachi
Kuala Lumpur Singapore Hong Kong Tokyo
Nairobi Dar es Salaam Cape Town
Melbourne Auckland

and associates in

Beirut Berlin Ibadan Mexico City Nicosia

First published 1981
Reprinted 1983

ISBN 0 19 831243 1

Printed in Great Britain at the University Press, Oxford
by Eric Buckley, Printer to the University

Contents

First words

What *is* poetry? It has almost as many definitions as it has people writing it because it is so wide-ranging and personal, yet exacting and impersonal, that it can reach out of every corner of every person's experience or imagination.

Some would call poetry fables or fictions—stories with a message that have no basis in actual truth or happening, a dream-like grouping of words and meanings; others say that it is any collection of words given in metrical language or rhythm, whether with some grand meanings or just the banality of a television commercial ('Don't go spare: polish your filthy floor with *Kare*!' or something like that); many have it that poetry is the expression of beautiful thoughts, though what the beauty is rather relies on the individual's likes and dislikes; still others would suggest that poetry is the giving of high-flown thoughts in appropriately high-flown language. Perhaps the best summary was that made by Coleridge, one of the finest English poets, when he stated that 'Prose = words in their best order; poetry = the *best* words in the best order.'

So it can be seen that anything to do with language can be construed as poetry or poetical if the reader or writer says that it is. This can best show itself in the fact that the shortest poem in the world consists of just a full stop (.) whilst the longest, an Indian poem written just before the time of Christ, has over three million words in it. St. Augustine thought poetry was evil, calling it 'the devil's wine' and yet some of the finest poetry is to be found in the Holy Bible. The Oracle at Delphi was said to speak in verse: prayers (and evil spells) are always made in poetical form. And of poets, Shelley said that they were the 'unacknowledged legislators of the world', Robert Burton said that all poets were mad and Robert Browning wrote that 'God is the perfect poet.' Attitudes towards poetry are massively broad.

The best description, which carries on from where Coleridge left off, is the one that states that poetry is the use of language to entertain, please, teach and explain, as exactly as possible and with the least wastage of words, the workings of human ideas and emotions. Above all, it is meant also to be fun—it may often be serious and deal with painful and sad events, but the underlying idea is that it should be enjoyed as an experience—much as one might enjoy going over Niagara Falls in a wooden barrel: you'd be scared stiff, but you'd still feel the thrill. The enjoyment comes at different levels of understanding for each reader, but that is the way it is. The poems in this book try to bring enjoyment: they may be studied, learnt and later quoted, but the main idea is understanding them, the ideas behind them and the men and women who wrote them, making this less of a chore and more of an experience shared.

Poems do not suddenly pop upon a poet's mind like a light-bulb switching on. They develop gradually from things that have been seen, sensed, felt or thought about; they have been worked upon many times, changing the words and, sometimes, the original idea too; they have been mulled over and tossed to and fro in the brain. Every poem is the result of a person's living and says something that that person wanted to say, either because he wanted to share it, or because it had to be written down to be cleared out of the system— much like talking about a worry with someone reduces that worry to a handle-able size. When anything from this book is read, these thoughts must be held in mind by the reader.

To help with the understanding of the poems, there are notes from page 155–176 which outline briefly what the poet is doing in each poem, and give a brief summary of the poet's life. Techniques and methods are discussed and another section explains these. For those who want to read more, there is a brief listing of easily obtained collections of verse by all the poets included in this anthology. Most of them are still living and writing. All of the poems are modern and therefore easy to get close to, to know.

This book is not intended merely for study. From it, one might hope, a desire to read more will spring up and maybe link itself with the writing of poetry and the listening to it—on record or in 'live' performance, for many poets give public readings of their work.

Finally . . . poetry is a part of literature and literature is made by people: it follows that literature is alive, for so are the people who make it. What this book has printed in it is not so much a large number of words as a collection of pieces of living activity, set to words and carrying emotions and happenings from the various writers' lives out to others—those whose eyes would go over the pages.   Editor

Headmaster: Modern Style

For Philip Hobsbaum

I

This leader's lonely, all right! He sees to that.
Inspectors, governors, parents, boys and staff—
His human instruments—are all shocked back
From the stunned area round him, sound of his voice.
Wag, wag, of tongue is his wig and his weapon
Raking a stamping ground
For his mannikin's hard-headed strut in a neat grey suit,
For those liquorice allsorts, his barrow-boy eyes
(Shrewdness and suspicion go on and off like traffic-lights)
For the maggot-twitch at the end of his almost endless nose.

II

What a nuisance the little man is!
If two stay behind, to paint scenery
And he offers to help
They toss for who does the painting and who listens to him.

III

'Snitch', the boys call him, 'Snitch' or 'Conk'.
'Rats,' he calls them, 'Slackers, Dirty Rats'.

IV

No Room for Gothic ghosts here
In the gleam of the public-urinal-type 1870 tiles —
There's a really up-to-date practical talking poltergeist
Resounds all day throughout the shameful building
That can't be prettied up, although they try:
It talks to the contractors' men on their small jobs —
He must slow them up.

V

And what does he talk about? Well, what was it?
Imagine a five act opera with only one voice,
Continuous recitativo secco monologue —
But in real life? And what is it all about?

It is for something and it isn't for you
It isn't something he'd want your opinion for
He's got it all worked out, he knows his line
Anecdote and anecdote and anecdote
To keep him talking, not to listen to you
Slugged into acquiescence by his knowing drone.

VI

He buzzes like pin-table-lights, flashing enormous scores
In disregard of what the ball is doing.
How does he keep it going?

Well, R.A.F. He was in the R.A.F.
A ground-staff commission in the R.A.F.
On heat with reminiscence on Battle-of-Britain day.
Knew how to get what they wanted, anything, any equipment
They knew their stuff, all right, when they occupied Germany
With nudges, winks, and Cockney chuckles.

And apparently spent all their time in the mess discussing
religion.
That put him on to Christ. That's where your ethics comes
from.
(He rehearses an operetta with a cane in his hand.)

Knows his way round any committee
Officials and contracts and regulations,
How to get round them, how to get praised for it.

VII

This poem goes on pattering just like he does.
This is the way to elicit expensive equipment.
The burgess are pleased to be stung for expensive equipment
(Quite a lot of the poor little wretches can't read)
New vistas in education, shining technical vistas

Showers and lathes and ropes and coats of paint
A new laboratory, new wood-work shop, new metal-work shop
Shelves in the library, elegant functional tombs
Where WILLIAM, BIGGLES, BUNTER rest in peace.

The boys should be grateful for all the equipment they're
    getting.

VIII

Let's turn aside
As Augustine might turn from a chapter on pride and
    concupiscence,
And consider poor Joe, Conk's deputy.

Joe does administration. It does for him. He's done by it.
Nothing comes right. He mutters about it.
Prometheus-Conk goes free. Joe gets the vultures.

Chief eunuch of the stock-room! Emperor of pen-nibs—
Footprints that vanish in the snow from Moscow!
And blotting-paper gone—to stuff the dykes?
The chalk they eat, the ink they drink.. . .

O the staff are a sore trial to poor old Joe!
They won't add their registers right. Their dinner-money's
    hopeless.
They will ask for stock on a Wednesday.
They send their classes down before the bell goes.. . .

Joe's tight face sits filling up the forms
And his small office shakes. A voice next door is sounding
About Christ and committees and polar exploration.

No doubt that Joe has still to be working, working, working.
And the Head to be talking, talking, talking.

IX

On Speech Day
The Chairman of the governors makes a speech.
An athlete makes a speech and gives out prizes.
The headmaster's speech is the longest.

Sea-shanties this year? No,
NON NOBIS DOMINE.

X

Let's finish this business off.
Let's take the backwardest class, 2E say,
Up the last stairs, to the Art Room. . . .

They are so eager to do something
That they stop being awkward, knocking things over, sit still
and attend.

Give out the clay. Never mind if they get it all over their
clothes,
All over the desks, all over the floor.

'Right! Now I want you to make a headmaster.'

They will solemnly prod into life long-snitched headmaster-
dolls.

Nothing crude like sticking pins?
Well all right, we will stick pins then, but also
Shove in chewed bubble-gum to make his eyes.

Give him a surplice of toffee-paper and hymn-book leaves.
Let bottle-tops stinking of yesterday's milk be gathered for his
medals.

Martin Bell

David Guest

Well O.K., he was wrong
Getting killed in Spain
Like that. Wal Hannington
Sat and tried to argue him out of going.
He was wrong, he was wrong.
The angel has not descended, the state
Hasn't the faintest chance of withering away,
And nobody is sure which way Hegel is up any more.
He was the greatest hero I've ever met because he was brave,
And would argue with anybody,

And could interest people because he was interested—
If he was so bloody interested he should have gone on talking,
    gone on talking,
Something might have been talked out.
Near to a saint, he should not have got himself killed,
Thereby making himself an ineffectual angel, a moth.
The Professor of economics was right:
He just couldn't keep still at a public meeting,
He would keep turning round and standing up to see what was
    happening and who was talking,
And this was probably how the bullet got him in the trenches
    at Jarama.

Martin Bell

Canal smell.

Canal smell. City that lies on the sea like a cork
of stone & gold, manifold throng your ghosts
of murdered & distraught.
St Mark's remains came here covered with pork,
stolen from Islam. Freedom & power, the Venetian hosts
cluttered blue seas where they sought

the wingèd lion on the conquered gates.
Doge followed Doge down down, the city floated.
Vassals drencht maps.
Fat popes & emperors to the high altar, hates
soothed into peace here. Nothing went unnoted
by the Patriarch perhaps

for a thousand years, when Henry struck his forehead
over his strange eyes & his monstrous beard
ah-ing 'This is too much.'
Canal smell, the Byzantine beauty of the dead,
with lovers arm in arm by the basin, weird
to Henry as such.

John Berryman

11

An Afternoon Visit

Deep she sank into Henry's mind, such years ago.
Now with her children & her lawyer-husband O
she is visited by Henry.
Burned she his gorgeous letters: he kept hers:
some assistant professor for the curious
& to become an associate

will utter with footnotes them, so all can read
& wonder at her spirit, tumultuous
as if a spirit could bleed,
now comes the visit mild & decorous
with Henry's child, & this will happen again
in the world of women & men.

A Henry James title.—Spare her, Mr Bones.
Preserve her the privacy which she now owns. –
—O yes, I will, I will.
After our deaths, then will the problem rise
when my blind eyes look into her blind eyes,
in the bronze damp & the chill.

25 June 68

John Berryman

In Memoriam (1914–1953)

I

Took my leave (last) five times before the end
and even past these precautions lost the end.
Oh, I *was* highlone in the corridor
    fifteen feet from his bed

where no other hovered, nurse or staff or friend,
and only the terrible breathing ever took place,
but trembling nearer after some small time
    I came on the tent collapsed

and silence—O unable to say when.
I stopped panicked a nurse, she a doctor
in twenty seconds, he pulled the plasticine,
    bent over, and shook his head at me.

Tubes all over, useless versus coma,
on the third day his principal physician
told me to pray he'd die, brain damage such.
    His bare stub feet stuck out.

II

So much for the age's prodigy, born one day
before I surfaced—when this fact emerged
Dylan grew stuffy and would puff all up
    rearing his head back and roar

'A little more—more—*respect* there, Berryman!'
Ah he had that,—so far ahead of me,
I half-adored him for his intricate booms & indecent tales
    almost entirely untrue.

Scorn bottomless for elders: we were twenty-three
but Yeats I worshipped: he was amused by this,
all day the day set for my tea with the Great Man
    he plotted to turn me up drunk.

Downing me daily at shove-ha'penny
with *English* on the thing. C—— would slump there
plump as a lump for hours, my word how that changed!
    Hard on her widowhood —

III

Apart a dozen years, sober in Seattle
'After many a summer' he intoned
putting out a fat hand. We shook hands.
    How very shook to see him.

His talk, one told me, clung latterly to Eden,
again & again of the Garden & the Garden's flowers,
not ever the Creator, only of that creation
    with a radiant will to go there.

13

I have sat hard for twenty years on this
mid potpals' yapping, and O I sit still still
though I quit crying that same afternoon
    of the winter of his going.

Scribbled me once, it's around somewhere or other,
word of their 'Edna Millay cottage' at Laugharne
saying come down to and disarm a while
    and down a many few.

O down a many few, old friend,
and down a many few.

John Berryman

Counting Small-Boned Bodies

Let's count the bodies over again.

If we could only make the bodies smaller,
The size of skulls,
We could make a whole plain white with skulls in the moon-
    light!

If we could only make the bodies smaller,
Maybe we could get
A whole year's kill in front of us on a desk!

If we could only make the bodies smaller,
We could fit
A body into a finger-ring, for a keepsake forever.

Robert Bly

Sleet Storm on the Merritt Parkway

I look out at the white sleet covering the still streets
As we drive through Scarsdale —
The sleet began falling as we left Connecticut,
And the winter leaves swirled in the wet air after cars
Like hands suddenly turned over in a conversation.
Now the frost has nearly buried the short grass of March.
Seeing the sheets of sleet untouched on the wide streets,
I think of the many comfortable homes stretching for miles,
Two and three stories, solid, with polished floors,
With white curtains in the upstairs bedrooms,
And small perfume flagons of black glass on the window sills,
And warm bathrooms with guest towels, and electric lights -
What a magnificent place for a child to grow up!
And yet the children end in the river of price-fixing,
Or in the snowy field of the insane asylum.
The sleet falls—so many cars moving toward New York—
Last night we argued about the Marines invading Guatemala
        in 1947,
The United Fruit Company had one water spigot for 200
        families,
And the ideals of America, our freedom to criticize,
The slave systems of Rome and Greece, and no one agreed.

Robert Bly

The Dead Seal near McClure's Beach

I

Walking north toward the point, I came on a dead seal. From a few feet away, he looks like a brown log. The body is on its back, dead only a few hours. I stand and look at him. There's a quiver in the dead flesh. My God he is still alive. A shock goes through me, as if a wall of my room had fallen away.

His head is arched back, the small eyes closed, the whiskers sometimes rise and fall. He is dying. This is the oil. Here on its back is the oil that heats our houses so efficiently. Wind blows fine sand back toward the ocean. The flipper near me lies folded over the stomach, looking like an unfinished arm, lightly glazed with sand at the edges. The other flipper lies half underneath. The seal's skin looks like an old overcoat, scratched here and there, by sharp mussel-shells maybe.. . .

I reach out and touch him. Suddenly he rears up, turns over, gives three cries, Awaark! Awaark! Awaark!—like the cries from Christmas toys. He lunges toward me. I am terrified and leap back, although I know there can be no teeth in that jaw. He starts flopping toward the sea. But he falls over, on his face. He does not want to go back to the sea. He looks up at the sky, and he looks like an old lady who has lost her hair.

He puts his chin back on the sand, rearranges his flippers, and waits for me to go. I go.

2

Today, I go back to say goodbye; he's dead now. But he's not— he's a quarter mile farther up the shore. Today he is thinner, squatting on his stomach, head out. The ribs show more—each vertebra on the back under the coat is now visible, shiny. He breathes in and out.

He raises himself up, and tucks his flippers under, as if to keep them warm. A wave comes in, touches his nose. He turns and looks at me—the eyes slanted, the crown of his head is like a black leather jacket. He is taking a long time to die. The whiskers white as porcupine quills, the forehead slopes ... goodbye brother, die in the sound of waves, forgive us if we have killed you, long live your race, your inner-tube race, so uncomfortable on land, so comfortable in the ocean. Be comfortable in death then, where the sand will be out of your nostrils, and you can swim in long loops through the pure death, ducking under as assassinations break above you. You don't want to be touched by me. I climb the cliff and go home the other way.

Robert Bly

Driving towards the Lac Qui Parle River

I

I am driving; it is dusk; Minnesota.
The stubble field catches the last growth of sun.
The soybeans are breathing on all sides.
Old men are sitting before their houses on car seats
In the small towns. I am happy,
The moon rising above the turkey sheds.

II

The small world of the car
Plunges through the deep fields of the night,
On the road from Willmar to Milan.
This solitude covered with iron
Moves through the fields of night
Penetrated by the noise of crickets.

III

Nearly to Milan, suddenly a small bridge,
And water kneeling in the moonlight.
In small towns the houses are built right on the ground;

The lamplight falls on all fours in the grass.
When I reach the river, the full moon covers it;
A few people are talking low in a boat.

Robert Bly

Coming In for Supper

It is lovely to follow paths in the snow made by human feet. The paths wind gaily around the ends of drifts, they rise and fall. How amazed I am, after working hard in the afternoon, that when I sit down at the table, with my elbows touching the elbows of my children, so much love flows out and around in circles. . . . The children have been working on a play.

Each child flares up as a small fire in the woods. . . . Biddy chortles over her new hair, curled for the first time last night, over her new joke song.

> *Yankee Doodle went to town,*
> *riding on a turtle,*
> *turned the corner just in time*
> *to see a lady's girdle. . . .*

Mary knows the inscription she wants on her coffin if she dies young, and says it:

> *Where the bee sucks there suck I*
> *In a cowslip's bell I lie. . . .*

She is obstinate and light at the same time, a heron who flies pulling long legs behind, or balances unsteadily on a stump, aware of all the small birds at the edge of the forest, where it is shadowy . . . longing to capture the horse with only one hair from its mane. . . .

Biddy can pick herself up and run over the muddy river bottom without sinking in; she already knows all about holding, and kisses each grownup carefully before going to bed; at the table she faces you laughing, bending over slightly

18

toward you, like a tree bent in wind, protective of this old shed she is leaning over. . . .

And all the books around on the walls are feathers in a great feather bed, they weigh hardly anything! Only the encyclopedias, left lying on the floor near the chair, contain the heaviness of the three-million-year-old life of the oyster-shell breakers, those long dusks—they were a thousand years long then—that fell over the valley from the cave mouth (where we sit). . . . The inventions found, then lost again . . . the last man killed by the flu who knew how to weave a pot of river clay the way the wasps do. . . . Now he is dead and only the wasps know in the long river-mud grief. The marmoset curls its toes once more around the slippery branch, remembering the furry chest of its mother, long since sunk into a hole that appeared in the afternoon. . . .

Dinner is finished, and the children pass out invitations composed with felt pens.

You are invited to 'The Thwarting of Captain Alphonse'

PRINCESS GARDINER : MARY BLY
CAPTAIN ALPHONSE : WESLEY RAY
AUNT AUGUST : BIDDY BLY
RAILWAY TRACK : NOAH BLY
TRAIN : SAM RAY

Costumes and Sets by Mary Bly and Wesley Ray
Free Will Offering Accepted

Robert Bly

The Horse That Had a Flat Tire

Once upon a valley
there came down
from some goldenblue mountains
a handsome young prince
who was riding
a dawncolored horse
named Lordsburg.

> I love you
> You're my breathing castle
> Gentle so gentle
> We'll live forever

In the valley
there was a beautiful maiden
whom the prince
drifted into love with
like a New Mexico made from
apple thunder and long
glass beads.

> I love you
> You're my breathing castle
> Gentle so gentle
> We'll live forever

The prince enchanted
the maiden
and they rode off
on the dawncolored horse
named Lordsburg
toward the goldenblue mountains.

> I love you
> You're my breathing castle
> Gentle so gentle
> We'll live forever

They would have lived
happily ever after
if the horse hadn't had
a flat tire
in front of a dragon's
house.

Richard Brautigan

The Chinese Checker Players

When I was six years old
I played Chinese checkers
      with a woman
who was ninety-three years old.
She lived by herself
in an apartment down the hall
      from ours.
We played Chinese checkers
every Monday and Thursday nights.
While we played she usually talked
about her husband
who had been dead for seventy years,
and we drank tea and ate cookies
      and cheated.

Richard Brautigan

On the Elevator
Going Down

A Caucasian gets on at
      the 17th floor.
He is old, fat and expensively
      dressed.

I say hello / I'm friendly.
      He says, 'Hi.'

Then he looks very carefully at
      my clothes.

I'm not expensively dressed.
I think his left shoe costs more
than everything I am wearing.

He doesn't want to talk to me
      any more.

I think that he is not totally aware
that we are really going down
and there are no clothes after you have
been dead for a few thousand years.

He thinks as we silently travel
down and get off at the bottom
      floor
that we are going separate
      ways.

Tokyo
June 4, 1976

Richard Brautigan

1939

Where the ball ran into the bushes,
And I was sent to find it, being
Useful for that more than to play their game,
I saw instead
This badge, from someone's brother, in
Some regiment of that war: a trophy
Begged for and polished, coveted certainly,
But lost now, slightly touched with dust already,
Yet shining still, under smooth leaves drab with dust.
I knew that people prized such trophies then,
It was the way of all of us. I might,
For no one looked, have taken it
For mine. I valued it. It shone
For me as much as anyone.
And yet some fear or honesty, some sense
It wasn't to be mine—it wasn't more —
Said No to all of this. Besides,
They shouted in the distance for their ball.
For once quite quickly, I
Made up my mind
And left the thing behind.

Alan Brownjohn

Office Party

We were throwing out small-talk
On the smoke-weary air,
When the girl with the squeaker
Came passing each chair.

She was wearing a white dress,
Her paper-hat was a blue
Crown with a red tassel,
And to every man who

Glanced up at her, she leant over
And blew down the hole,
So the squeaker inflated
And began to unroll.

She stopped them all talking
With this trickery,
And she didn't leave out anyone
Until she came to me.

I looked up and she met me
With a half-teasing eye
And she took a mild breath and
Went carefully by,

And with odd concentration
To the next man she went,
And squawked out the instrument
To its fullest extent.

And whether she passed me
Thinking that it would show
Too much favour to mock me
I never did know —

Or whether her withholding
Was her cruelty,
And it was that she despised me,
I couldn't quite see —

So it could have been discretion,
And it could have been disgust,
But it was quite unequivocal,
And suffer it I must:

All I know was: she passed me,
Which I did not expect
—And I've never so craved for
Some crude disrespect.

Alan Brownjohn

A 202

This coarse road, my road, struggles out
South-east across London, an exhausted
Grey zigzag of stubborn, unassimilable
    Macadam, passing hoardings pasted

With blow-ups of cricket journalists, blackened
And not-quite-Georgian terraces,
Shagged-out Greens of geraniums and
    Floral coats-of-arms, lost pieces

Of genteel façade behind and above
Lyons' shopfronts and 'Pullum Promotions',
—Journeying between wired-off bombed lots glossy
    With parked Consuls, making diversions

Round bus depots and draggled estates
In circumlocutory One-Ways,
Netting aquaria in crammed pet store windows,
    Skirting multi-racial bingo queues,

And acquiring, for its self-hating hoard, old black-railed
Underground bogs advising the Seamen's Hospital,
'Do-it-yourself' shops, 'Funerals and Monuments', and
    Victorian Charrington pubs. All

Along its length it despoils, in turn, a sequence
Of echoless names: Camberwell, Peckham,
New Cross Gate; places having no recorded past
    Except in histories of the tram.

It takes out, in cars, arterial affluence
At week-ends, returning it as bad blood
To Monday mornings in town. It is altogether
    Like a vein travelled by hardy diseases, an aged

Canal dredgeable for bodies left behind
On its soulless travels: Sixty-Nine,
Thirty-Six, One-Eight-Five. It takes no clear
    Attitude anyone could easily define

So as to resist or admire it. It seems to hate you
Possessively, want to envelop you in nothing
Distinguishable or distinguished, like its own
    Smothered slopes and rotting

Valleys. This road, generally, is one for
The long-defeated; and turns any ironic
Observer's tracer-isotope of ecology,
    Sociology, or hopeful manic

Verse into a kind of mere
Nosing virus itself. It leaves its despondent, foul
And intractable deposit on its own
    Banks all the way like virtually all

Large rivers, particularly the holy ones, which it
Is not. It sees little that deserves to be undespised.
It only means well in the worst of ways.
    How much of love is much less compromised?

Alan Brownjohn

Song of the Dying Gunner AA1

Oh mother my mouth is full of stars
As cartridges in the tray
My blood is a twin-branched scarlet tree
And it runs all runs away.

Oh 'Cooks to the galley' is sounded off
And the lads are down in the mess
But I lie done by the forrard gun
With a bullet in my breast.

Don't send me a parcel at Christmas time
Of socks and nutty and wine
And don't depend on a long weekend
By the Great Western Railway line.

Farewell, Aggie Weston, the Barracks at Guz,
Hang my tiddley suit on the door
I'm sewn up neat in a canvas sheet
And I shan't be home no more.

[HMS *Glory*]

AA1: Anti-Aircraft Gunner, 1st Class
Aggie Weston: the familiar term used by sailors to describe the hostels
  founded in many seaports by Dame Agnes Weston
Guz: naval slang for Devonport
tiddley suit: sailor's best shore-going uniform with gold badges

Charles Causley

John Polruddon

John Polruddon
All of a sudden
Went out of his house one night,

    When a privateer
    Came sailing near
    Under his window-light.

They saw his jugs
His plates and mugs,
His hearth as bright as brass,

    His gews and gaws
    and kicks and shaws
    All through their spying-glass.

They saw his wine
His silver shine
They heard his fiddlers play.

    'Tonight,' they said,
    'Out of his bed
    Polruddon we'll take away.'

And from a skiff
They climbed the cliff
And crossed the salt-wet lawn,

    And as they crept
    Polruddon slept
    The night away to dawn.

'In air or ground
What is that sound?'
Polruddon said, and stirred,

    They breathed, 'Be still,
    It was the shrill
    Of the scritch-owl you heard.'

'O yet again
I hear it plain,
But do I wake or dream?

    'In morning's fog
    The otter-dog
    Is whistling by the stream.

'Now from the sea
What comes for me
Beneath my window dark?'

    'Lie still, my dear,
    All that you hear
    Is the red fox's bark.'

Swift from his bed
Polruddon was sped
Before the day was white,

    And head and feet
    Wrapped in a sheet
    They bore him down the height.

And never more
Through his own door
Polruddon went nor came,

    Though many a tide
    Has turned beside
    The cliff that bears his name.

On stone and brick
Was ivy thick,
And the grey roof was thin,

    And winter's gale
    With fists of hail
    Broke all the windows in.

The chimney-crown
It tumbled down
And up grew the green,

Till on the cliff
It was as if
A house had never been.

But when the moon
Swims late or soon
Across St Austell Bay,

What sight, what sound
Haunts air and ground
Where once Polruddon lay?

It is the high
White scritch-owl's cry,
The fox as dark as blood,

And on the hill
The otter still
Whistles beside the flood.

John Polruddon's house was on the cliff over Pentewan, in south
Cornwall. The story of his disappearance dates from early
Tudor times.

Charles Causley

The Animal's Carol

Christus natus est! the cock
Carols on the morning dark.

Christ is born

Quando? croaks the raven stiff
Freezing on the broken cliff.

When?

Hoc nocte, replies the crow
Beating high above the snow.

This night

Ubi? ubi? booms the ox
From its cavern in the rocks.

Where?

Bethlehem, then bleats the sheep
Huddled on the winter steep.

Bethlehem

Quomodo? the brown hare clicks,
Chattering among the sticks.

How?

Humiliter, the careful wren
Thrills upon the cold hedge-stone.

Humbly

Cur? cur? sounds the coot
By the iron river-root.

Why?

Propter homine, the thrush
Sings on the sharp holly-bush.

For the sake of man

Cui? cui? rings the chough
On the strong, sea-haunted bluff.

To whom?

Mary! Mary! calls the lamb
From the quiet of the womb.

Mary

Praeterea ex quo? cries
The woodpecker to pallid skies.

Who else?

Joseph, breathes the heavy shire
Warming in its own blood-fire.

Joseph

Ultime ex quo? the owl
Solemnly begins to call.

Who above all?

De Deo, the little stare   Of God
Whistles on the hardening air.

Pridem? pridem? the jack snipe   Long ago?
From the stiff grass starts to pipe.

Sic et non, answers the fox   Yes and no
Tiptoeing the bitter lough.

Quomodo hoc scire potest?   How do I know this?
Boldly flutes the robin redbreast.

Illo in eandem, squeaks   By going there
The mouse within the barley-sack.

Quae sarcinae? asks the daw   What luggage?
Swaggering from head to claw.

Nulla res, replies the ass,   None
Bearing on its back the Cross.

Quantum pecuniae? shrills   How much money?
The wandering gull about the hills.

Ne nummum quidem, the rook   Not a penny
Caws across the rigid brook.

Nulla resne? barks the dog   Nothing at all?
By the crumbling fire-log.

Nil nisi cor amans, the dove   Only a loving heart
Murmurs from its house of love.

Gloria in Excelsis! Then
Man is God, and God is Man.

Charles Causley

The Wealth

When he returned to New York in December 1965, he figured his stay
would be a brief one, that he'd earn $25,000 if he was lucky, enough
to live comfortably in England. Instead, he earned ten times that
much. The success—and the terrors that accompanied it—had begun.
Paul Cowan, on Paul Simon *Rolling Stone, 1 July, 1976*

If I prove nothing to you, it's my fault.
The planet's round and greedy.
This song-infatuated globe can't handle it,
In love with rip-off and reward.

It is an old perdition to be rich,
An old displeasure to be seen dismayed
With what you wanted, when, having it, it hurts
Or turns against you in the night.

The last day of December '65
I got a letter from your Uncle Sam.
I'd thought of him as one of the good guys,
Stern, dressed in a dollar, but on our side.

By then I was in two minds.
A lot of people were dying, like clichés.
I wasn't even an American.
Gabe read my papers over, then we hit the town.

The Go-Go girls brought New Year in
Dancing on our table   *Snoopy, hang on!*
I didn't lose my mind in drink. I sulked.
The night-club scooped me up and took me home.

I walked to the bus depot in the snow.
January. They took us to Cleveland.
I didn't want to go. Nick said, 'Go. Buy time.'
We walked around, afraid in underpants.

Faced with a form, I opted for the Coastguard,
'And don't let me see any damn fool
Write "coastguard", gentlemen', yelled a sailor.
There were six-foot-six football giants

Who fainted away in the lottery
Of the blood-test. I wouldn't have missed it,
Not for anything. I didn't faint. I felt —
I felt *proud*. And then *I* couldn't pee in the cup.

A doctor said, if he was me, he'd go back
To Scotland. 'Randall Jarrell', I said. '*Huh?*'
The man next in line pushed me, and asked
If I was 'some kinda coward'. 'Yes', I said.

I said I wasn't an American.
You can't say that to a man in blue jockey-shorts
Who'd been insisting on the Marine Corps.
'A medical is close enough', I said.

If that man went to Vietnam, I hope
He didn't die, or kill anyone,
Or help reduce thin children to
An orphanage of ash.

We used to visit in Peninsula, Ohio,
A precious farmhouse on a wooded hill.
I planted corn, walked on an Indian trail,
James Fenimore Cooper for a day.

The poems in my head were facing west
Towards a continental summer.
I won't deny it. The Stars and Stripes
On a blue autumn day is quite something.

But then, so was I, in casuals,
Fit and young, athletic, frivolous —
As if nobody knew me then—one round year married,
My wife in tears at having to go home so soon.

I liked old villages with soldier-statued squares
Where I could stand and feel like Robert Lowell.
Still there, and probably the same,
Each with its radical son and its casualty.

States of long trains and the astounding autumn.
I squeaked before your laws, reduced
To nakedness, my penis in a cup
Refusing Uncle Sam his specimen of me —

My health, portrayed in Akron's
Tax-paid chemicals, *Cutty Sark*,
Upper New York State wine—oh, Liz, *your* wine!—
And food bought in the Kroger Store.

We shipped aboard SS *United States*.
I went home on a name
With nothing like enough
To live on comfortably.

I felt like a Jew, at Hamburg
On a boat bound for America,
A Jew at Hamburg, 1932,
And wept for laws, but not for me, civilian,

Writing poetry, seasick on the North Atlantic,
Reading *Henderson the Rain King*
And *For the Union Dead*.
I wanted it torpedoed, by the British.

But, for you, a terror was beginning . . .
Such is the magnitude of song.
An American critic, writing of
An English poet who thinks himself classical

Has said of tenderness, it is
'The social face of self-pity.'
If I say, tenderly, I am afraid,
Who do I fear, or what? *Horror*. 'The wealth! The wealth!'

America, I admit it. You've beaten me.
I'll end up in a regiment of *foederati*
To be led forever by a minor Belisarius
Against my kin in the forests of Europe.

Our armoured herds are grazing on the map.
And so are theirs. I write this for *détente*,
Which, as ever, should be personal.
One false move then, I'd have no right to speak.

In your culture, I am a barbarian,
But I'm that here, and everywhere,
Lulled by alien rites, lullabyed with remorse
Here on the backstreets of the universe.

Douglas Dunn

Young Women in Rollers

Because it's wet, the afternoon is quiet.
Children pacified with sweets inside
Their small houses, stroke travelling cats
From the kingdom of dustbins and warm smells.

Young women come to visit their married friend.
Waiting for their hair to set beneath thin scarves,
They walk about in last year's fashions,
Stockingless, in coats and old shoes.

They look strong, white-legged creatures
With nothing to do but talk of what it is to love
And sing the words softly to the new tunes.
The type who burst each other's blackheads

In the street and look in handbag mirrors
While they walk, not talking of the weather;
Who call across the street they're not wearing knickers,
But blush when they pass you alone.

This time they see me at my window, among books,
A specimen under glass, being protected,
And laugh at me watching them.
They minuet to Mozart playing loudly

On the afternoon Third. They mock me thus,
They mime my softness. A landlord stares.
All he has worked for is being destroyed.
The slum rent-masters are at one with Pop.

The movements they imagine go with minuet
Stay patterned on the air. I can see soot,
It floats. The whiteness of their legs has changed
Into something that floats, become like cloth.

They disappear into the house they came to visit.
Out of the open door rush last year's hits,
The music they listen to, that takes up their time
In houses that are monuments to entertainment.

I want to be touched by them, know their lives,
Dance in my own style, learn something new,
At night, I even dream of ideal communities.
Why do they live where they live, the rich and the poor?

Tonight, when their hair is ready, after tea,
They'll slip through laws and the legs of policemen.
I won't be there, I'll be reading books elsewhere.
There are many worlds, there are many laws.

Douglas Dunn

Mugging

I

Tonite I walked out of my red apartment door on East tenth
street's dusk—
Walked out of my home ten years, walked out in my honking
neighborhood
Tonite at seven walked out past garbage cans chained to con-
crete anchors
Walked under black painted fire escapes, giant castiron plate
covering a hole in ground
—Crossed the street, traffic lite red, thirteen bus roaring by
liquor store,
past corner pharmacy iron grated, past Coca Cola & My-Lai
posters fading scraped on brick
Past Chinese Laundry wood door'd, & broken cement stoop
steps For Rent hall painted green & purple Puerto Rican
style
Along E. 10th's glass splattered pavement, kid blacks & Span-
ish oiled hair adolescents' crowded house fronts—
Ah, tonite I walked out on my block NY City under humid
summer sky Halloween,
thinking what happened Timothy Leary joining brain police
for a season?
thinking what's all this Weathermen, secrecy & selfrighteous-
ness beyond reason—F.B.I. plots?

Walked past a taxicab controlling the bottle strewn curb—

past young fellows with their umbrella handles & canes
leaning against ravaged Buick

—and as I looked at the crowd of kids on the stoop—a boy
stepped up, put his arm around my neck

tenderly I thought for a moment, squeezed harder, his um-
brella handle against my skull,

and his friends took my arm, a young brown companion
tripped his foot 'gainst my ankle—

as I went down shouting Om Ah Hūm to gangs of lovers on
the stoop watching

slowly appreciating, why this is a raid, these strangers mean
strange business

with what—my pockets, bald head, broken-healed-bone leg,
my softshoes, my heart –

Have they knives? Om Ah Hūm—Have they sharp metal
wood to shove in eye ear ass? Om Ah Hūm

& slowly reclined on the pavement, struggling to keep my
woolen bag of poetry address calendar & Leary-lawyer
notes hung from my shoulder

dragged in my neat orlon shirt over the crossbar of a broken
metal door

dragged slowly onto the fire-soiled floor an abandoned store,
laundry candy counter 1929—

now a mess of papers & pillows & plastic covers cracked cock-
roach-corpsed ground—

my wallet back pocket passed over the iron foot step guard

and fell out, stole by God Muggers' lost fingers, Strange—

Couldn't tell—snakeskin wallet actually plastic, 70 dollars
my bank money for a week,

old broken wallet—and dreary plastic contents—Amex card
& Manf. Hanover Trust Credit too—business card from
Mr. Spears British Home Minister Drug Squad—my
draft card—membership ACLU & Naropa Institute
Instructor's identification

Om Ah Hūm I continued chanting Om Ah Hūm

Putting my palm on the neck of an 18 year old boy fingering
my back pocket crying 'Where's the money'

'Om Ah Hūm there isn't any'

My card Chief Boo-Hoo Neo American Church New Jersey
& Lower East Side
Om Ah Hūṁ—what not forgotten crowded wallet—Mobil
Credit, Shell? old lovers addresses on cardboard pieces,
booksellers calling cards—
—'Shut up or we'll murder you'—'Om Ah Hūṁ take it easy'
Lying on the floor shall I shout more loud?—the metal door
closed on blackness
one boy felt my broken healed ankle, looking for hundred
dollar bills behind my stocking weren't even there—a third
boy untied my Seiko Hong Kong watch rough from right
wrist leaving a clasp-prick skin tiny bruise
'Shut up and we'll get out of here'—and so they left,
as I rose from the cardboard mattress thinking Om Ah Hūṁ
didn't stop em enough,
the tone of voice too loud—my shoulder bag with 10,000
dollars full of poetry left on the broken floor—

Nov. 2, 1974

II

Went out the door dim eyed, bent down & picked up my
glasses from step edge I placed them while dragged in
the store—looked out—
Whole street a bombed-out face, building rows' eyes & teeth
missing
burned apartments half the long block, gutted cellars,
hallways' charred beams
hanging over trash plaster mounded entrances, couches &
bedsprings rusty after sunset
Nobody home, but scattered stoopfuls of scared kids frozen
in black hair
chatted giggling at house doors in black shoes, families
cooked For Rent some six story houses mid the street's
wreckage
Nextdoor Bodega, a phone, the police? 'I just got mugged'
I said
to man's face under fluorescent grocery light tin ceiling –
puffy, eyes blank & watery, sickness of beer kidney and
language tongue

thick lips stunned as my own eyes, poor drunken Uncle
    minding the store!
O hopeless city of idiots empty staring afraid, red beam top'd
    car at street curb arrived –
'Hey maybe my wallet's still on the ground got a flashlight?'
Back into the burnt-doored cave, & the policeman's grey
    flashlight broken no eyebeam—
'My partner all he wants is sit in the car never get out Hey Joe
    bring your flashlight –'
a tiny throwaway beam, dim as a match in the criminal dark
'No I can't see anything here' . . . 'Fill out this form'
Neighborhood street crowd behind a car 'We didn't see nothing'
Stoop young girls, kids laughing 'Listen man last time I
    messed with them see this –'
rolled up his skinny arm shirt, a white knife scar on his brown
    shoulder
'Besides we help you the cops come don't know anybody we
    all get arrested
go to jail I never help no more mind my own business everytime'
'Agh!' upstreet think 'Gee I don't know anybody here ten
    years lived half block crost Avenue C
and who knows who?' – passing empty apartments, old lady
    with frayed paper bags
sitting in the tin-boarded doorframe of a dead house.
December 10, 1974

Allen Ginsberg

Father Death Blues

    Hey Father Death, I'm flying home
    Hey poor man, you're all alone
    Hey old daddy, I know where I'm going

    Father Death, Don't cry any more
    Mama's there, underneath the floor
    Brother Death, please mind the store

Old Aunty Death   Don't hide your bones
Old Uncle Death   I hear your groans
O Sister Death   how sweet your moans

O Children Deaths go breathe your breaths
Sobbing breasts'll ease your Deaths
Pain is gone, tears take the rest

Genius Death   your art is done
Lover Death your body's gone
Father Death   I'm coming home

Guru Death your words are true
Teacher Death I do thank you
For inspiring me to sing this Blues

Buddha Death, I wake with you
Dharma Death, your mind is true
Sangha Death, we'll work it through

Suffering is what was born
Ignorance made me forlorn
Tearful truths I cannot scorn

Father Breath once more farewell
Birth you gave was no thing ill
My heart is still, as time will tell.

July 8, 1976 (over Lake Michigan)

Allen Ginsberg

41

Written on Hotel Napkin: Chicago Futures

Wind mills churn on Windy City's
      rooftops   Antennae
        collecting electric
above thick-loamed gardens
     on Playboy Tower
Merchandise Mart's compost
          privies
    supply nightsoil for Near North Side's
         back Gardens
Cabbages, celery & cucumbers
    sprout in Mayor Daley's
        frontyard
    rich with human waste –
Bathtub beer like old days
Backyard Mary Jane like
      old days,
Sun reflectors gather heat
    in rockpile collectors
     under apartment walls
Horses graze in Parks &
    streets covered with grass
Mafia Dons shovel earth
     & bury Cauliflower
      leaves
Old gangsters & their sons
    tending grapevines

mid-March 1975

Allen Ginsberg

An Airstrip in Essex, 1960

It is a lost road into the air.
It is a desert
among sugar beets.
The tiny wings
of the Spitfires of nineteen-forty-one
flake in the mud of the Channel.

Near the road a brick pillbox
totters under a load of grass,
where Home Guards waited
in the white fogs of the invasion winter.

Goodnight, old ruined war.

In Poland the wind rides on a jagged wall.
Smoke rises from the stones; no, it is mist.

Donald Hall

The Old Pilot's Death

He discovers himself on an old airfield.
He thinks he was there before,
but rain has washed out the lettering of a sign.
A single biplane, all struts and wires,
stands in the long grass and wildflowers.
He pulls himself into the narrow cockpit
although his muscles are stiff
and sits like an egg in a nest of canvas.
He sees that the machine gun has rusted.
The glass over the instruments
has broken, and the red arrows are gone
from his gas gauge and his altimeter.
When he looks up, his propeller is turning,
although no one was there to snap it.

He lets out the throttle. The engine catches
and the propeller spins into the wind.
He bumps over holes in the grass,
and he remembers to pull back on the stick.
He rises from the land in a high bounce
which gets higher, and suddenly he is flying again.
He feels the old fear, and rising over the fields
the old gratitude. In the distance, circling
in a beam of late sun like birds migrating,
there are the wings of a thousand biplanes.
He banks and flies to join them.

in memory of Philip Thompson, d. 1960

The Farm

Standing on top of the hay
in a good sweat,
I felt the wind from the lake,
dry on my back,
where the chaff
grew like the down on my face.

At night on the bare boards
of the kitchen,
we stood while the old man
in his nightshirt gummed
the stale crusts
of his bread and milk.

Up on the gray hill
behind the barn, the stones
had fallen away
where the Pennacook marked
a way to go
south from the narrow river.

By the side of the lake
my dead uncle's rowboat rots

in heavy bushes.
Slim pickerel glint
in the water. Black horned pout
doze on the bottom.

Donald Hall

Maple Syrup

August, goldenrod blowing. We walk
into the graveyard, to find
my grandfather's grave. Ten years ago
I came here last, bringing
marigolds from the round garden
outside the kitchen.
I didn't know you then.
     We walk
among carved names that go with photographs
on top of the piano at the farm:
Keneston, Wells, Fowler, Batchelder, Buck.
We pause at the new grave
of Grace Fenton, my grandfather's
sister. Last summer
we called on her at the nursing home,
eighty-seven, and nodding
in a blue housedress. We cannot find
my grandfather's grave.
     Back at the house
where no one lives, we potter
and explore the back chamber
where everything comes to rest: spinning wheels,
pretty boxes, quilts,
bottles, books, albums of postcards.
Then with a flashlight we descend
firm steps to the root cellar—black,
cobwebby, huge,
with dirt floors and fieldstone walls,

and above the walls, holding the hewn
sills of the house, enormous
granite foundation stones.
Past the empty bins
for squash, apples, carrots, and potatoes,
we discover the shelves for canning, a few
pale pints
of tomato left, and—what
is this?—syrup, maple syrup
in a quart jar, syrup
my grandfather made twenty-five
years ago
for the last time.
                    I remember
coming to the farm in March
in sugaring time, as a small boy.
He carried the pails of sap, sixteen-quart
buckets, dangling from each end
of a wooden yoke
that lay across his shoulders, and emptied them
into a vat in the saphouse
where fire burned day and night
for a week.
                 Now the saphouse
tilts, nearly to the ground,
like someone exhausted
to the point of death, and next winter
when snow piles three feet thick
on the roofs of the cold farm,
the saphouse will shudder and slide
with the snow to the ground.
                      Today
we take my grandfather's last
quart of syrup
upstairs, holding it gingerly,
and we wash off twenty-five years
of dirt, and we pull
and pry the lid up, cutting the stiff,
dried rubber gasket, and dip our fingers

in, you and I both, and taste
the sweetness, you for the first time,
the sweetness preserved, of a dead man
in his own kitchen,
giving us
from his lost grave the gift of sweetness.

Donald Hall

The Grauballe Man

[handwritten: Consisting of similes]
[handwritten: Poet imagines man in bog.]

As if he had been poured
in tar, he lies
on a pillow of turf
and seems to weep

the black river of himself.
The grain of his wrists
is like bog oak,
the ball of his heel

like a basalt egg.
His instep has shrunk
cold as a swan's foot
or a wet swamp root.

His hips are the ridge
and purse of a mussel,
his spine an eel arrested
under a glisten of mud.

The head lifts,
the chin is a visor
raised above the vent
of his slashed throat

[handwritten: Shocking reaction]

that has tanned and toughened.
The cured wound
opens inwards to a dark
elderberry place.

[handwritten: image of leather]

Who will say 'corpse'
to his vivid cast?
Who will say 'body'
to his opaque repose?

And his rusted hair,
a mat unlikely
as a foetus's.
I first saw his twisted face

in a photograph,
a head and shoulder
out of the peat,
bruised like a forceps baby,

but now he lies
perfected in my memory,
down to the red horn
of his nails,

hung in the scales
with beauty and atrocity:
with the Dying Gaul
too strictly compassed

on his shield,
with the actual weight
of each hooded victim,
slashed and dumped.

Seamus Heaney

The Outlaw

Kelly's kept an unlicensed bull, well away
From the road: you risked fine but had to pay

The normal fee if cows were serviced there.
Once I dragged a nervous Friesian on a tether

Down a lane of alder, shaggy with catkin,
Down to the shed the bull was kept in.

I gave Old Kelly the clammy silver, though why
I could not guess. He grunted a curt 'Go by

Get up on that gate'. And from my lofty station
I watched the business-like conception.

The door, unbolted, whacked back against the wall,
The illegal sire fumbled from his stall

Unhurried as an old steam engine shunting.
He circled, snored and nosed. No hectic panting,

Just the unfussy ease of a good tradesman;
Then an awkward, unexpected jump, and

His knobbled forelegs straddling her flank,
He slammed life home, impassive as a tank,

Dropping off like a tipped-up load of sand.
'She'll do,' said Kelly and tapped his ash-plant

Across her hindquarters. 'If not, bring her back.'
I walked ahead of her, the rope now slack

While Kelly whooped and prodded his outlaw
Who, in his own time, resumed the dark, the straw.

Seamus Heaney

Seamus Heaney   6 stanzas.

Follower

My father worked with a horse-plough,
His shoulders globed like a full sail strung   simile
Between the shafts and the furrow.   Rhyme
The horses strained at his clicking tongue.

An expert. He would set the wing
And fit the bright steel-pointed sock.   Rhyme.
The sod rolled over without breaking.
At the headrig, with a single pluck

Of reins, the sweating team turned round
And back into the land. His eye
Narrowed and angled at the ground,
Mapping the furrow exactly.

I stumbled in his hob-nailed wake,
Fell sometimes on the polished sod;
Sometimes he rode me on his back
Dipping and rising to his plod.

I wanted to grow up and plough,
To close one eye, stiffen my arm.
All I ever did was follow
In his broad shadow round the farm.

I was a nuisance, tripping, falling,
Yapping always. But today   roles reversed.
It is my father who keeps stumbling
Behind me, and will not go away.

Seamus Heaney

A New Song

I met a girl from Derrygarve
And the name, a lost potent musk,
Recalled the river's long swerve,
A kingfisher's blue bolt at dusk

And stepping stones like black molars
Sunk in the ford, the shifty glaze
Of the whirlpool, the Moyola
Pleasuring beneath alder trees.

And Derrygarve, I thought, was just,
Vanished music, twilit water,
A smooth libation of the past
Poured by this chance vestal daughter.

But now our river tongues must rise
From licking deep in native haunts
To flood, with vowelling embrace,
Demesnes staked out in consonants.

And Castledawson we'll enlist
And Upperlands, each planted bawn—
Like bleaching-greens resumed by grass—
A vocable, as rath and bullaun.

Seamus Heaney

3. Orange Drums, Tyrone, 1966
from Singing School

The lambeg balloons at his belly, weighs
Him back on his haunches, lodging thunder
Grossly there between his chin and his knees.
He is raised up by what he buckles under.

Each arm extended by a seasoned rod,
He parades behind it. And though the drummers
Are granted passage through the nodding crowd
It is the drums preside, like giant tumours.

To every cocked ear, expert in its greed,
His battered signature subscribes 'No Pope'.
The pigskin's scourged until his knuckles bleed.
The air is pounding like a stethoscope.

Seamus Heaney

Mantle

Mantle ran so hard, they said,
he tore his legs to pieces.
What is this but spirit?

I prayed for him to quit before
his lifetime dropped below .300.
But he didn't, and it did.

He makes Brylcreem commercials now,
models with open mouths draped around him
as they never were in Commerce, Oklahoma,

where the sandy-haired, wide-shouldered boy
stood up against his barn,
lefty for an hour (Ruth, Gehrig),

then righty (DiMaggio),
as his father winged them in,
and the future blew toward him,

now a fastball, now a slow
curve hanging
like a model's smile.

William Heyen

Pet's Death

A truck crept
into our driveway,
but caught him
in its rear wheels.

We buried him
under the twin maples
in our back yard.
Let this be a lesson,

my father said,
but for nights I heard
my dog clawing his way out until,
one morning, his grave

was sunken.
But it was only rain
during the night,
my father said, and threw down

a few shovels of dirt.
But I continued
to dream him:
he was dirty and wet,

but he slept
as he slept in his shed,
curled in his corner
like a possum.

William Heyen

Spring

For I have seen
honeysuckle twine
the moss-green rib-
cage of a fawn.

William Heyen

Driving at Dawn

Driving at dawn past Buffalo
we point to steel mills' stacks
reddening the sky as though
they threaten to set it afire. Hereabouts
soot rains steadily on the shacks
of steelmen and their ashen wives,
once sparks themselves in other lives
that burned a while, but then went out.

A limbo of gray trees and grass, then
A few miles more
and roadsides are green again
under the sun. This arsonist,
rising with matches in his fist,
glaring our windshield's ash on fire,
burns again for the steelmen
who burned like hell for their women.

William Heyen

Legend of the Tree at the Center of the World

Blizzard. The great oak's roots
snapped from sand.
Wind blew it across the Lake Ronkonkoma ice
where, between shores, it settled, like a forest.

The next was a bell-clear morning:
Sun glittered its limbs until
green leaves appeared from Never.
Then the lake's roof fell.

All night the water swirled. Gods
battled beneath the ice. Moon
plunged near and shook loose showers
of arrows. That morning was the first Spring.

William Heyen

Worming at Short Beach

At Short Beach, reaching
    almost to the horizon, successions
        of sandbars lay bared

to the low tide, the furthest,
    toward which I walked
        over the wormgrounds,

toward which I waded
    through shallow sluices of channel,
        almost indistinct, and now blurred,

a small island of the mind
    I've tried to touch,
        define, and hold.

But I remember, as gulls worked
   the water's edge, ripped
      hermits from houses of shell,

or in my wake split
   the razors I threw aside,
      I remember, my back against

the sun's blaze, worming that far bar,
   forking close to clumps of sawgrass,
      turning the wet sand over,

breaking the worms' domains
   open to the dark sheen
      of my shadow.

My fork rasped against
   the shells of softclams
      that sprayed small geysers

as I dug, and the wind
   was a thin whisper of scythes
      over the waves. And now,

all this from a long time ago
   is almost lost
      and goes nowhere, except deeper,

year by year. But this was the way
   when I worked that far bar,
      the light fell: the sandworms

were blood-red in my shadow,
   as I forked them
      into my shadow.

William Heyen

Son Dream

I went looking for my son
and found him in the grass,
prone, his chin in his hands,
watching a black bull snake.
I said, 'Be careful, my son,
anything can happen.'
Beside him, somehow, a possum
rolled from under leaves, bared its teeth
but licked his ear. I said
'Watch out.' At that
a coon appeared,
touched my son's nose
gently with its pink fingers,
and lay down beside him.
I stood in my tracks, afraid, until
a wolf rose from the grass,
and licked my son's forehead.
My heart pumped the word 'rabid'
into the space behind my eyes.
'He is only twelve, Lord,' I prayed.
The gun was soundless when I fired.
The snake, the animals
began to shine, to shine.
My son and I walked home, holding hands.
He said, 'I love you,'
but when I looked back he lay in the grass,
his chin cupped in his hands,
the snake and animals a shining
circle around him.

William Heyen

A Bedtime Story

Once upon a time there was a person
Almost a person

Somehow he could not quite see
Somehow he could not quite hear
He could not quite think
Somehow his body, for instance,
Was intermittent

He could see the bread he cut
He could see the letters of words he read
He could see the wrinkles on handskin he looked at
Or one eye of a person
Or an ear, or a foot, or the other foot
But somehow he could not quite see

Nevertheless the Grand Canyon spread wide open
Like a surgical operation for him
But somehow he had only half a face there
And somehow his legs were missing at the time
And though somebody was talking he could not hear
Though luckily his camera worked O.K.
The sea-bed lifted its privacy
And showed its most hidden fish-thing
He stared he groped to feel
But his hands were funny hooves just at the crucial moment
And though his eyes worked
Half his head was jellyfish, nothing could connect
And the photographs were blurred
A great battleship broke in two with a boom
As if to welcome his glance
An earthquake shook a city onto its people
Just before he got there
With his rubber eye his clockwork ear
And the most beautiful girls
Laid their faces on his pillow staring him out
But somehow his eyes were in the wrong way round

He laughed he whispered but somehow he could not hear
He gripped and clawed but somehow his fingers would not
    catch
Somehow he was a tar-baby
Somehow somebody was pouring his brains into a bottle
Somehow he was already too late
And was a pile of pieces under a blanket
And when the seamonster surfaced and stared at the rowboat
Somehow his eyes failed to click
And when he saw the man's head cleft with a hatchet
Somehow staring blank swallowed his entire face
Just at the crucial moment
Then disgorged it again whole
As if nothing had happened

So he just went and ate what he could
And did what he could
And grabbed what he could
And saw what he could

Then sat down to write his autobiography
But somehow his arms were just bits of stick
Somehow his guts were an old watch-chain
Somehow his feet were two old postcards
Somehow his head was a broken windowpane

'I give up,' he said. He gave up.

Creation had failed again.

Ted Hughes

Tractor

The tractor stands frozen—an agony
To think of. All night
Snow packed its open entrails. Now a head-pincering gale,
A spill of molten ice, smoking snow,
Pours into its steel.
At white heat of numbness it stands
In the aimed hosing of ground-level fieriness.

It defies flesh and won't start.
Hands are like wounds already
Inside armour gloves, and feet are unbelievable
As if the toe-nails were all just torn off.
I stare at it in hatred. Beyond it
The copse hisses—capitulates miserably
In the fleeing, failing light. Starlings,
A dirtier sleetier snow, blow smokily, unendingly, over
Towards plantations Eastward.
All the time the tractor is sinking
Through the degrees, deepening
Into its hell of ice.

The starting lever
Cracks its action, like a snapping knuckle.
The battery is alive—but like a lamb
Trying to nudge its solid-frozen mother—
While the seat claims my buttock-bones, bites
With the space-cold of earth, which it has joined
In one solid lump.

I squirt commercial sure-fire
Down the black throat—it just coughs.
It ridicules me—a trap of iron stupidity
I've stepped into. I drive the battery
As if I were hammering and hammering
The frozen arrangement to pieces with a hammer
And it jabbers laughing pain-crying mockingly
Into happy life.

And stands
Shuddering itself full of heat, seeming to enlarge slowly
Like a demon demonstrating
A more-than-usually-complete materialisation—
Suddenly it jerks from its solidarity
With the concrete, and lurches towards a stanchion
Bursting with superhuman well-being and abandon
Shouting Where Where?

Worse iron is waiting. Power-lift kneels,
Levers awake imprisoned deadweight,
Shackle-pins bedded in cast-iron cow-shit.
The blind and vibrating condemned obedience
Of iron to the cruelty of iron,
Wheels screeched out of their night-locks—

Fingers
Among the tormented
Tonnage and burning of iron

Eyes
Weeping in the wind of chloroform

And the tractor, streaming with sweat,
Raging and trembling and rejoicing.

Ted Hughes

Wodwo

What am I? Nosing here, turning leaves over
Following a faint stain on the air to the river's edge
I enter water. What am I to split
The glassy grain of water looking upward I see the bed
Of the river above me upside down very clear
What am I doing here in mid-air? Why do I find
this frog so interesting as I inspect its most secret
interior and make it my own? Do these weeds
know me and name me to each other have they
seen me before, do I fit in their world? I seem
separate from the ground and not rooted but dropped
out of nothing casually I've no threads
fastening me to anything I can go anywhere
I seem to have been given the freedom
of this place what am I then? And picking
bits of bark off this rotten stump gives me
no pleasure and it's no use so why do I do it
me and doing that have coincided very queerly
But what shall I be called am I the first
have I an owner what shape am I what
shape am I am I huge if I go
to the end on this way past these trees and past these trees
till I get tired that's touching one wall of me
for the moment if I sit still how everything
stops to watch me I suppose I am the exact centre
but there's all this what is it roots
roots roots roots and here's the water
again very queer but I'll go on looking

Ted Hughes

The Burrow Wolf

A kind of wolf lives in the moon's holes
Waiting for meteorites to score goals.

The meteorites come down blazing with velocity
And this wolf greets them with a huge grin of ferocity.

Whack to the back of his gullet go those glowing rocks
And the wolf's eyes start clean out of his head on eleven
    inch stalks.

But only for a moment, then he smiles and swallows
And shuts his eyes as over the melt of marshmallows.

Rockets nosediving on to the moon for modern adventures
Will have to reckon with those abnormal dentures.

Many a spaceman in the years to come
Will be pestled with meteorites in that horny tum.

If he does not dive direct into those jaws
He may well wander in there after a short pause.

For over the moon general madness reigns—
Bad when the light waxes, worse when it wanes—

And he might lunatically mistake this wolf for his wife.
So the man in the moon ended *his* life.

Ted Hughes

A Solstice

Drip-tree stillness. Spring-feeling elation
Of mid-morning oxygen. There is a yeasty simmering
Over the land – all compass points are trembling,
Bristling with starlings, hordes out of Siberia,
Bubbly and hopeful.

We stand in the mist-rawness

63

Of the sodden earth. Four days to Christmas.
We can hear the grass seeping.
                              Now a wraith-smoke
Writhes up from a far field, condenses
On a frieze of goblin hedge-oaks, sizzling
Like power-pylons in mist.

We ease our way into this landscape.
Casual midnightish draughts, in the soaking stillness.
Itch of starlings is everywhere.
                              The gun
Is old, rust-ugly, single-barrelled, borrowed
For a taste of English sport. And you have come
From eighteen years Australian estrangement
And twelve thousand miles in thin air
To walk again on the small hills of the West,
In the ruby and emerald lights, the leaf-wet oils
Of your memory's masterpiece.
                              Hedge-sparrows
Needle the bramble-mass undergrowth
With their weepy warnings.
                              You have the gun.
We harden our eyes. We are alert.
The gun-muzzle is sniffing. And the broad land
Tautens into wilder, nervier contrasts
Of living and unliving. Our eyes feather over it
As over a touchy detonator.

Bootprints between the ranks of baby barley
Heel and toe we go
Narrowed behind the broad gaze of the gun
Down the long woodside. I am your dog.

Now I get into the wood. I push parallel
And slightly ahead of you—the idea
Is to flush something for the gun's amusement.
I go delicate. I don't want to panic
My listeners into a crouch-freeze.
I want them to keep their initiative
And slip away, confident, impudent,
Out across your front.

                    Pigeons, too far,
Burst up from under the touch
Of our furthest listenings. A bramble
Claws across my knee, and a blackbird
Five yards off explodes its booby-trap
Shattering wetly
Black and yellow alarm-dazzlings, and a long string
Of fireworks down the wood. It settles
To a hacking chatter and that blade-ringing—
Like a flint on an axe-head.
                    I wait.
That startled me too.
I know I am a Gulliver now
Tied by my every slightest move
To a thousand fears. But I move—
And a jay, invisibly somewhere safe,
Starts pretending to tear itself in half
From the mouth backward. With three screams
It scares itself to silence.
                    The whole wood
Has hidden in the wood. Its mossy tunnels
Seem to age as we listen. A raven
Dabs a single charcoal toad-croak
Into the finished picture.

                    I come out
To join you in the field. We need a new plan
To surprise something.
                    But as I come over the wire
You are pointing, silent.
I look. One hundred yards
Down the woodside, somebody
Is watching us.

A strangely dark fox
Motionless in his robe of office
Is watching us. It is a shock.

Too deep in the magic wood, suddenly
We meet the magician.

Then he's away—
A slender figurine, dark and witchy,
A rocking nose-down lollop, and the load of tail
Floating behind him, over the swell of faint corn
Into the long arm of woodland opposite.

The gun does nothing. But we gaze after
Like men who have been given a secret sign.
We are studying the changed expression
Of that straggle of scrub and poor trees
Which is now the disguise of a fox.

And the gun is thinking. The gun
Is working its hunter's magic.
It is transforming us, there in the dull mist,
To two suits of cold armour—
Empty of all but a strange new humming,
A mosquito of primaeval excitements.

And as we start to walk out over the field
The gun smiles.

The fox will be under brambles.
He has set up all his antennae,
His dials are glowing and quivering,
Every hair adjusts itself
To our coming.

Will he wait in the copse
Till we've made our move, as if this were a game
He is interested to play?
Or has he gone through and away over further fields,
Or down and into the blueish mass and secrecy
Of the main wood?

Under a fat oak, where the sparse copse
Joins the main wood, you lean in ambush.
Well out in the field, talking to air
Like quiet cogs, I stroll to the top of the strip—
Then pierce it, clumsy as a bullock, a careless trampling
Like purposeless machinery, towards you,
Noisy enough for you to know

Where not to point your blind gun.

Somewhere between us
The fox is inspecting me, magnified.
And now I tangle all his fears with a silence,
Then a sudden abrupt advance, then again silence,
Then a random change of direction—

And almost immediately—
Almost before I've decided we are serious—
The blast wall hits me, the gun bang bursts
Like a paper bag in my face,
The whole day bursts like a paper bag—

But a new world is created instantly
With no visible change.

I pause. I call. You do not answer.
Everything is just as it had been.
The corroded blackberry leaves,
The crooked naked trees, fingering sky
Are all the usual careful shapes
Of the usual silence.

I go forward. And now I see you,
As if you had missed,
Leaning against your tree, casual.

But between us, on the tussocky ground,
Somebody is struggling with something.
An elegant gentleman, beautifully dressed,
Is struggling there, tangled with something,
And biting at something
With his flashing mouth. It is himself
He is tangled with. I come close
As if I might be of help.
But there is no way out.
It is himself he is biting,
Bending his head far back, and trying
To bite his shoulder. He has no time for me.
Blood beneath him is spoiling

The magnificent sooted russet

Of his overcoat, and the flawless laundering
Of his shirt. He is desperate
To get himself up on his feet,
And if he could catch the broken pain
In his teeth, and pull it out of his shoulder,
He still has some hope, because
The long brown grass is the same
As it was before, and the trees
Have not changed in any way,
And the sky continues the same—

It is doing the impossible deliberately
To set the gun-muzzle at his chest
And funnel that sky-bursting bang
Through a sudden blue pit in his fur
Into the earth beneath him.

He cannot believe it has happened.

His chin sinks forward, and he half-closes his mouth
In a smile
Of ultimate bitterness,
And half closes his eyes
In a fineness beyond pain—

And it is a dead fox in the dank woodland.
And you stand over him
Meeting your first real Ancient Briton
In eighteen years.
And I stand awake—as one wakes
From what feels like a cracking blow on the head.

That second shot has ruined his skin.
We chop his tail off
Thick and long as a forearm, and black.
Then bundle him and his velvet legs
His bag of useless jewels,
The phenomenal technology inside his head,
Into a hole, under a bulldozed stump,
Like picnic rubbish. There the memory ends.

We must have walked away.

Ted Hughes

A motorbike

We had a motorbike all through the war
In an outhouse—thunder, flight, disruption
Cramped in rust, under washing, abashed, outclassed
By the Brens, the Bombs, the Bazookas elsewhere.

The war ended, the explosions stopped.
The men surrendered their weapons
And hung around limply.
Peace took them all prisoner.
They were herded into their home towns.
A horrible privation began
Of working a life up out of the avenues
And the holiday resorts and the dance-halls.

Then the morning bus was as bad as any labour truck,
The foreman, the boss, as bad as the S.S.
And the ends of the street and the bends of the road
And the shallowness of the shops and the shallowness of
    the beer
And the sameness of the next town
Were as bad as electrified barbed wire.
The shrunk-back war ached in their testicles
And England dwindled to the size of a dog-track.

So there came this quiet young man
And he bought our motorbike for twelve pounds.
And he got it going, with difficulty.
He kicked it into life—it erupted
Out of the six year sleep, and he was delighted.

A week later, astride it, before dawn,
A misty frosty morning,
He escaped

Into a telegraph pole
On the long straight west of Swinton.

Ted Hughes

Cock-Crows

I stood on a dark summit, among dark summits—
Tidal dawn splitting heaven from earth,
The oyster opening to taste gold.

And I heard the cockcrows kindling in the valley
Under the mist—
They were sleepy,
Bubbling deep in the valley cauldron.

Then one or two tossed clear, like soft rockets
And sank back again dimming.

Then soaring harder, brighter, higher
Tearing the mist,
Bubble-glistenings flung up and bursting to light
Brightening the undercloud,
The fire-crests of the cocks—the sickle shouts,
Challenge against challenge, answer to answer,
Hooking higher,
Clambering up the sky as they melted,
Hanging smouldering from the night's fringes.

Till the whole valley brimmed with cockcrows,
A magical soft mixture boiling over,
Spilling and sparkling into other valleys

Lobbed-up horse-shoes of glow-swollen metal
From sheds in back-gardens, hen-cotes, farms
Sinking back mistily

Till the last spark died, and embers paled

And the sun climbed into its wet sack
For the day's work

While the dark rims hardened
Over the smoke of towns, from holes in earth.

Ted Hughes

The River that is East

1

Buoys begin clanging like churches
And peter out. Sunk to the gunwhales
In their shapes tugs push upstream.
A carfloat booms down, sweeping past
Illusory suns that blaze in puddles
On the shores where it rained, past the Navy Yard,
Under the Williamsburg Bridge
That hangs facedown from its strings
Over which the Jamaica Local crawls,
Through white-winged gulls which shriek
And flap from the water and sideslip in
Over the chaos of illusions, dangling
Limp red hands, and screaming as they touch.

2

A boy swings his legs from the pier,
His days go by, tugs and carfloats go by,
Each prow pushing a whitecap. On his deathbed
Kane remembered the abrupt, missed Grail
Called Rosebud, Gatsby must have thought back
On his days digging clams in Little Girl Bay
In Minnesota, Nick fished in dreamy Michigan,
Gant had his memories, Griffeths, those
Who went baying after the immaterial
And whiffed its strange dazzle in a blonde
In a canary convertible, who died
Thinking of the Huck Finns of themselves
On the old afternoons, themselves like this boy
Swinging his legs, who sees the *Ile de France*
Come in, and wonders if in some stateroom
There is not a sick-hearted heiress sitting
Drink in hand, saying to herself his name.

3

A man stands on the pier.
He has long since stopped wishing his heart were full
Or his life dear to him.
He watches the snowfall hitting the dirty water.
He thinks: Beautiful. Beautiful.
If I were a gull I would be one with white wings,
I would fly out over the water, explode, and
Be beautiful snow hitting the dirty water.

4

And thou, River of Tomorrow, flowing . . .
We stand on the shore, which is mist beneath us,
And regard the onflowing river. Sometimes
It seems the river stops and the shore
Flows into the past. Nevertheless, its leaked promises
Hopping in the bloodstream, we strain for the future,
Sometimes even glimpse it, a vague, scummed thing
We dare not recognize, and peer again
At the cabled shroud out of which it came,
We who have no roots but the shifts of our pain,
No flowering but our own strange lives.

What is this river but the one
Which drags the things we love,
Processions of debris like floating lamps,
Towards the radiance in which they go out?
No, it is the River that is East, known once
From a high window in Brooklyn, in agony—river
On which a door locked to the water floats,
A window sash paned with brown water, a whisky crate,
Barrel staves, sun spokes, feathers of the birds,
A breadcrust, a rat, spittle, butts, and peels,
The immaculate stream, heavy, and swinging home again.

Galway Kinnell

Spindrift

1

On this tree thrown up
From the sea, its tangle of roots
Letting the wind go through, I sit
Looking down the beach: old
Horseshoe crabs, broken skates,
Sand dollars, sea horses, as though
Only primeval creatures get destroyed,
At chunks of sea-mud still quivering,
At the light as it glints off the water
And the billion facets of the sand,
At the soft, mystical shine the wind
Blows over the dunes as they creep.

2

Sit down
By the clanking shore
Of this bitter, beloved sea,

Pluck sacred
Shells from the icy surf,
Fans of gold light, sunbursts,

Lift one to the sun
As a sign you accept to go,
As bid, to the shrine of the dead,

And as it blazes
See the lost life within
Alive again in the fate-shine.

3

This little bleached root
Drifted from some foreign shore,
Brittle, cold, practically weightless,

If anything is dead, it is,
This castout worn
To the lost grip it always essentially was.

If it has lost hold
It at least keeps the wild
Shape of what it held,

And it remains the hand
Of that gravel, one of the earth's
Wandering icons of 'to have.'

4

I sit listening
To the surf as it falls,
The power and inexhaustible freshness of the sea,
The suck and inner boom
As a wave tears free and crashes back
In overlapping thunders going away down the beach.

It is the most we know of time,
And it is our undermusic of eternity.

5

I think of how I
Sat by a dying woman,
Her shell of a hand,
Wet and cold in both of mine,
Light, nearly out, existing as smoke,
I sat in the glow of her wan, absorbed smile.

6

Under the high wind
That moans in the grass
And whistles through crabs' claws
I sit holding this little lamp,
This icy fan of the sun.

Across gull tracks
And wind ripples in the sand
The wind seethes. My footprints

Slogging for the absolute
Already begin vanishing.

7

What does he really love,
That old man,
His wrinkled eyes
Tortured by smoke,
Walking in the ungodly
Rasp and cackle of old flesh?

The swan dips her head
And peers at the mystic
In-life of the sea,
The gull drifts up
And eddies towards heaven,
The breeze in his arms . . .

Nobody likes to die
But an old man
Can know
A kind of gratefulness
Towards time that kills him,
Everything he loved was made of it.

In the end
What is he but the scallop shell
Shining with time like any pilgrim?

Galway Kinnell

Tree from Andalusia

1

This old bleached tree
Dumped on the Sagaponack beach . . .
The wind has lifted and only seethes
Far up among the invisible stars,
Yet I hear in the limbs a tragic voice,
As once on Ferry Street, at night,
Among *to let* signs and closed wholesalers,
From some loft I heard a phrase of jazz,
y recuerdo una brisa triste por los olivos.

2

The wind starts fluting
In our teeth, in our ears,
It whines down the harmonica
Of the fingerbones, moans at the skull . . .

Blown on by their death
The things on earth whistle and cry out.
Nothing can keep still. Only the wind.

Galway Kinnell

The Bear

1

In late winter
I sometimes glimpse bits of steam
coming up from
some fault in the old snow
and bend close and see it is lung-colored
and put down my nose
and know
the chilly, enduring odor of bear.

2

I take a wolf's rib and whittle
it sharp at both ends
and coil it up
and freeze it in blubber and place it out
on the fairway of the bears.

And when it has vanished
I move out on the bear tracks,
roaming in circles
until I come to the first, tentative, dark
splash on the earth.

And I set out
running, following the splashes
of blood wandering over the world.
At the cut, gashed resting places
I stop and rest,
at the crawl-marks
where he lay out on his belly
to overpass some stretch of bauchy ice
I lie out
dragging myself forward with bear-knives in my fists.

3

On the third day I begin to starve,

at nightfall I bend down as I knew I would
at a turd sopped in blood,
and hesitate, and pick it up,
and thrust it in my mouth, and gnash it down,
and rise
and go on running.

4

On the seventh day,
living by now on bear blood alone,
I can see his upturned carcass far out ahead, a scraggled,
steamy hulk,
the heavy fur riffling in the wind.

I come up to him
and stare at the narrow-spaced, petty eyes,
the dismayed
face laid back on the shoulder, the nostrils
flared, catching
perhaps the first taint of me as he
died.

I hack
a ravine in his thigh, and eat and drink,
and tear him down his whole length
and open him and climb in
and close him up after me, against the wind,
and sleep.

5

And dream
of lumbering flatfooted
over the tundra,
stabbed twice from within,
splattering a trail behind me,
splattering it out no matter which way I lurch,
no matter which parabola of bear-transcendence,
which dance of solitude I attempt,
which gravity-clutched leap,
which trudge, which groan.

6

Until one day I totter and fall—
fall on this
stomach that has tried so hard to keep up,
to digest the blood as it leaked in,
to break up
and digest the bone itself: and now the breeze
blows over me, blows off
the hideous belches of ill-digested bear blood
and rotted stomach
and the ordinary, wretched odor of bear,

blows across
my sore, lolled tongue a song
or screech, until I think I must rise up
and dance. And I lie still.

7

I awaken I think. Marshlights
reappear, geese
come trailing again up the flyway.
In her ravine under old snow the dam-bear
lies, licking
lumps of smeared fur
and drizzly eyes into shapes
with her tongue. And one
hairy-soled trudge stuck out before me,
the next groaned out,
the next,
the next,
the rest of my days I spend
wandering: wondering
what, anyway,
was that sticky infusion, that rank flavor of blood, that
    poetry, by which I lived?

Galway Kinnell

Philip Larkin

Mr Bleaney

'This was Mr Bleaney's room. He stayed
The whole time he was at the Bodies, till
They moved him.' Flowered curtains, thin and frayed,
Fall to within five inches of the sill,

Whose window shows a strip of building land,
Tussocky, littered. 'Mr Bleaney took
My bit of garden properly in hand.'
Bed, upright chair, sixty-watt bulb, no hook

Behind the door, no room for books or bags—
'I'll take it.' So it happens that I lie
Where Mr Bleaney lay, and stub my fags
On the same saucer-souvenir, and try

Stuffing my ears with cotton-wool, to drown
The jabbering set he egged her on to buy.
I know his habits—what time he came down,
His preference for sauce to gravy, why

He kept on plugging at the four aways—
Likewise their yearly frame: the Frinton folk
Who put him up for summer holidays,
And Christmas at his sister's house in Stoke.

But if he stood and watched the frigid wind
Tousling the clouds, lay on the fusty bed
Telling himself that this was home, and grinned,
And shivered, without shaking off the dread

That how we live measures our own nature,
And at his age having no more to show
Than one hired box should make him pretty sure
He warranted no better, I don't know.

Philip Larkin

The Explosion

On the day of the explosion
Shadows pointed towards the pithead:
In the sun the slagheap slept.

Down the lane came men in pitboots
Coughing oath-edged talk and pipe-smoke,
Shouldering off the freshened silence.

One chased after rabbits; lost them;
Came back with a nest of lark's eggs;
Showed them; lodged them in the grasses.

So they passed in beards and moleskins,
Fathers, brothers, nicknames, laughter,
Through the tall gates standing open.

At noon, there came a tremor; cows
Stopped chewing for a second; sun,
Scarfed as in a heat-haze, dimmed.

The dead go on before us, they
Are sitting in God's house in comfort,
We shall see them face to face—

Plain as lettering in the chapels
It was said, and for a second
Wives saw men of the explosion

Larger than in life they managed—
Gold as on a coin, or walking
Somehow from the sun towards them,
One showing the eggs unbroken.

Philip Larkin

Going, Going

I thought it would last my time—
The sense that, beyond the town,
There would always be fields and farms,
Where the village louts could climb
Such trees as were not cut down;
I knew there'd be false alarms

In the papers about old streets
And split-level shopping, but some
Have always been left so far;
And when the old parts retreat
As the bleak high-risers come
We can always escape in the car.

Things are tougher than we are, just
As earth will always respond
However we mess it about;
Chuck filth in the sea, if you must:
The tides will be clean beyond.
—But what do I feel now? Doubt?

Or age, simply? The crowd
Is young in the M1 café;
Their kids are screaming for more—
More houses, more parking allowed,
More caravan sites, more pay.
On the Business Page, a score

Of spectacled grins approve
Some takeover bid that entails
Five per cent profit (and ten
Per cent more in the estuaries): move
Your works to the unspoilt dales
(Grey area grants)! And when

You try to get near the sea
In summer . . .

It seems, just now,
To be happening so very fast;
Despite all the land left free
For the first time I feel somehow
That it isn't going to last,

That before I snuff it, the whole
Boiling will be bricked in
Except for the tourist parts—
First slum of Europe: a role
It won't be so hard to win,
With a cast of crooks and tarts.

And that will be England gone,
The shadows, the meadows, the lanes,
The guildhalls, the carved choirs.
There'll be books; it will linger on
In galleries; but all that remains
For us will be concrete and tyres.

Most things are never meant.
This won't be, most likely: but greeds
And garbage are too thick-strewn
To be swept up now, or invent
Excuses that make them all needs.
I just think it will happen, soon.

Philip Larkin

Death of a Ferrari
in memoriam 840 HYK

I

It was made for the manager of Crockford's,
    Driven in a Monte Carlo Rally,
Owned by a salesman, later, at Maranello's,
    A retired colonel, then me.

I couldn't afford that wastrel elegance.
    I could scarcely carry
The seven-foot, iron exhaust system
    When it cracked, and broke, in Leeds.

I loved its worn, greyed ivory leather,
    The petrol-blue of its hide.
It growled along at 104
    With its bad brakes, and its leaking seal.

I can hear now that famous,
    Belly-flustering Ferrari roar
Bounced back off the wall of the underpass
    One night, in Piccadilly. It was like the blitz.

All right. So the door was rusted,
    Smoke came out of the dashboard wires
The first time I drove it on the M4.
    Who cares? It was a major car.

    II

It didn't crash on the motorway,
    Or blow up at 150.
It didn't burn itself out down a cliff
    Taking a bend too fast, in Scotland.

It was ditched in a car-park
    On Willesden Green.
So under the Civic Amenities Act 1967
    Section No. 20

Removal and Disposal of Abandoned Vehicles
    The Transport and Cleansing Division
Of the London Borough of Brent
    Will sell it for scrap.

Some other owner is responsible,
    The next sucker in the line.
But I feel tonight a remote sense of guilt
    Mixed with a tinge of outrage

To think of the rationality of that great engine
    Ripped into shreds,
The camshaft smashed, the radial tires torn loose,
    And the little dancing horse stripped from the grill.

It had electric windows, in 1961.
    It had the original radio, with its aerial.
It could out-accelerate any car in Europe.
    They don't come off the floor like that any more.

George MacBeth

Poem for Breathing

Trudging through drifts along the hedge, we
Probe at the flecked, white essence with sticks. Across
    The hill field, mushroom-brown in
The sun, the mass of the sheep trundle
As though on small wheels. With a jerk, the farmer

Speaks, quietly pleased. *Here's one.* And we
Hunch round while he digs. Dry snow flies like castor
    Sugar from the jabbing edge
Of the spade. The head rubs clear first, a
Yellow cone with eyes. The farmer leans, panting,

On the haft. *Will you grab him from the*
Front? I reach down, grope for greasy fur, rough, neat
    Ears. I grip at shoulders, while
He heaves at the coarse, hairy
Backside. With a clumsy lug, it's up, scrambling

    For a hold on the white, soft grass. It
Stares round, astonished to be alive. Then it

Runs, like a rug on legs, to
Join the shy others. Ten dark little
Pellets of dung steam in the hole, where it lay

Dumped, and sank in. *You have to probe with*
The pole along the line of the rest of the
    Hedge. They tend to be close. We
Probe, floundering in Wellingtons, breath
Rasping hard in the cold. The released one is

All right. He has found his pen in the
Sun. I dig in the spade's thin haft, close to barbed
    Wire. Someone else speaks. *Here's*
Another. And it starts again. The
Rush to see, the leaning sense of hush, and the

Snow-flutter as we grasp for the quick
Life buried in the ivory ground. *There were*
    Ninety eight, and I counted
Ninety five. That means one more. And I
Kneel to my spade, feeling the chill seep through my

Boots. The sun burns dark. I imagine
The cold-worn ears, the legs bunched in the foetus
    Position for warmth. I smell
The feathery, stale white duvet, the
Hot air from the nostrils, burning upwards. And

I crouch above the sheep, hunched in its
Briar bunk below the hedge. From the field, it
    Hears the bleat of its friends, their
Far joy. It feels only the cushions
Of frost on its frozen back. I breathe, slowly,

Trying to melt that hard-packed snow. I
Breathe, melting a little snow with my breath. If
    Everyone in the whole
World would breathe here, it might help. Breathe
Here a little, as you read, it might still help.

George MacBeth

George MacBeth

The Land-mine

It fell when I was sleeping. In my dream
    It brought the garden to the house
And let it in. I heard no parrot scream
    Or lion roar, but there were flowers
And water flowing where the cellared mouse
Was all before. And air moved as in bowers

Of cedar with a scented breath of smoke
    And fire. I rubbed scales from my eyes
And white with brushed stone in my hair half-woke
    In fear. I saw my father kneel
On glass that scarred the ground. And there were flies
Thick on that water, weeds around his heel

Where he was praying. And I knew that night
    Had cataracted through the wall
And loosed fine doors whose hinges had been tight
    And made each window weep glass tears
That clawed my hands. I climbed through holes. My hall
Where I had lain asleep with stoppered ears

Was all in ruins, planted thick with grime
    Of war. I walked as if in greaves
Through fire, lay down in gutters choked with lime
    And spoke for help. Alas, those birds
That dived in light above me in the leaves
Were birds of prey, and paid no heed to words.

Now I was walking, wearing on my brow
    What moved before through fireless coal
And held my father's head. I touch it now
    And feel my dream go. And no sound
That flying birds can make, or burrowing mole,
Will bring my garden back, or break new ground.

The war is over and the mine has gone
    That filled the air with whinnying fire

And no more nights will I lie waiting on
    Cold metal or cold stone to freeze
Before it comes again. That day of ire,
If it shall come, will find me on my knees.

George MacBeth

A True Story

When the British Association
For the Advancement of Science held
Its Annual Meeting one year in
    East Anglia no-one could

Think what to feed them on. It appeared
From previous experience in
County Durham that members consumed
    An enormous quantity

Of sandwiches. How were the hundreds
Of visiting scientists to be
Fed? The problem was finally solved
    By the inspiration of

A Norfolk poacher who suggested
At a public meeting in the Town
Hall at Norwich the employment of
    Their local pest the Coypu

Rat. He claimed that between two layers
Of freshly cut bread a thick slice of
Coypu tasted quite delicious. And
    It proved so. At any rate

The sandwiches were bought and eaten
In extraordinarily large
Numbers. The plain bread seemed to set off
    The unusual taste of

The dead rodent. Indeed a group of
Younger men from the Biology
Section dissected the furry beasts
    With a view to assessing

Just why. Altogether it was 'a
Great success for the quality of
Willingness to experiment' as
    'The Countryman' aptly said.

George MacBeth

Marshall

It occurred to Marshall
that if he were a vegetable, he'd
be a bean. Not
one of your thin, stringy
green beans, or your

dry, marbly
Burlotti beans. No, he'd be
a broad bean,
a rich, nutritious,
meaningful bean,

alert for advantages,
inquisitive with potatoes,
mixing with every kind
and condition of vegetable,
and a good friend

to meat and lager. Yes, he'd
leap from his huge
rough pod with a loud
popping sound
into the pot: always

in hot water
and out of it with a soft
heart inside
his horny carapace. He'd
carry the whole

world's hunger on
his broad shoulders, green
with best butter
or brown with gravy. And if
some starving Indian saw his

flesh bleeding
when the gas was turned on
or the knife went in
he'd accept the homage and prayers,
and become a god, and die like a man,

which, as things were, wasn't so easy.

George MacBeth

Open Day at Porton

These bottles are being filled with madness,
A kind of liquid madness concentrate
Which can be drooled across the land
Leaving behind a shuddering human highway . . .

A welder trying to eat his arm.

Children pushing stale food into their eyes
To try to stop the chemical spectaculars
Pulsating inside their hardening skulls.

A health visitor throwing herself downstairs,
Climbing the stairs, throwing herself down again
Shouting: Take the nails out of my head.

There is no damage to property.

Now, nobody likes manufacturing madness,
But if we didn't make madness in bottles
We wouldn't know how to deal with bottled madness.

We don't know how to deal with bottled madness.

We all really hate manufacturing madness
But if we didn't make madness in bottles
We wouldn't know how to be sane.

Responsible madness experts assure us
Britain would never be the first
To uncork such a global brainquake.

But suppose some foreign nut sprayed Kent
With his insanity aerosol . . .
Well, there's only one answer to madness.

Adrian Mitchell

Dumb Insolence

I'm big for ten years old
Maybe that's why they get at me

Teachers, parents, cops
Always getting at me

When they get at me

I don't hit em
They can do you for that

I don't swear at em
They can do you for that

I stick my hands in my pockets
And stare at them

And while I stare at them
I think about sick

They call it dumb insolence

They don't like it
But they can't do you for it

I've been done before
They say if I get done again

They'll put me in a home
So I do dumb insolence

Adrian Mitchell

Old Age Report

When a man's too ill or old to work
We punish him.
Half his income is taken away
Or all of it vanishes and he gets pocket-money.

We should reward these tough old humans for surviving,
Not with a manager's soggy handshake
Or a medal shaped like an alarm clock—
No, make them a bit rich,
Give the freedom they always heard about
When the bloody chips were down
And the blitz or the desert
Swallowed their friends.

Retire, retire into a fungus basement
Where nothing moves except the draught
And the light and dark grey figures
Doubling their money on the screen;
Where the cabbages taste like the mummy's hand
And the meat tastes of feet;
Where there is nothing to say except:
'Remember?' or 'Your turn to dust the cat.'

To hell with retiring. Let them advance.
Give them the money they've always earned
Or more—and let them choose.
If Mr Burley wants to be a miser,
Great, let the moneybags sway and clink for him,
Pay him a pillowful of best doubloons.
So Mrs Wells has always longed to travel?
Print her a season ticket to the universe,
Let her slum-white skin
Be tanned by a dozen different planets.
We could wipe away some of their worry,
Some of their pain—what I mean
Is so bloody simple:
The old people are being robbed
And punished and we ought
To be letting them out of their cages
Into green spaces of enchanting light.

Adrian Mitchell

Adrian Mitchell

Lady Macbeth in the Saloon Bar Afterwards

It was all going surprisingly well—
Our first school matinee and we'd got up to
My sleepwalking scene with the minimum of titters . . .
Right, enter me, somnambulistically.
One deep sigh. Then some lout tosses
A banana on to the forestage.
It got a round? Darling, it got a thunderstorm!
Of course, we carried on, but suddenly
We had a panto audience
Yelling out: 'Look out! He's behind you!'
Murders, battles, Birnham Wood, great poetry—
All reduced to mockery.
The Bard upstaged by a banana.
Afterwards we had a flaming row in the Grenville
About just who should have removed it
And just when—
One of the servants, obviously.
And ever since, at every performance:
Enter myself in those exquisite ribbons
And—plomp—a new out-front banana.
Well, yes, it does affect *all* our performances
But actually, *they* seem to love it.
And how, now Ben's in Canada
Doling out Wesker to the Eskimos,
Can we decide who *exits with banana*?
You can't expect me to parade down there,
Do a sort of boob-baring curtsey and announce:
'Is this a banana that I see before me?'
Anyway, darling, we may have egg on our faces—
But we've got a hit on our hands.

Adrian Mitchell

Old Crock

I am the very last astronaut, listen:
I send back messages from obscure planets;
smoke rises from the burning leaves,
something goes liquid beyond my reach.

I am the very last astronaut, listen:
I came here, surfacing like a whale
through oceans alchemists made real.

Listen: space-bugs scrape around the cockpit,
terror leaks in, spilling about the controls;
lice block the air tubes, eat into my brain.

I have forgotten my space pills, I
might explode.

About the brain: most is machinery anyway.
No worry there; only the memory now
feels soft and edible.

My only fear: that the lice might nest there,
eat out the shapes I've carried with me.
Still now I sense my loneliness breaking.

Now someone else has arrived here,
space-jaunted naked, sits invisible here.
I'm obsolete, he tells me, holds up a mirror.

I am the very last astronaut, listen:
skull-white I grin,
skull-white and obviously mad.

Outside there are children playing
like this blackness were a park,
dancing, their songs numerical—

I am too many centuries old.

In the brain-pan bits of machinery float,
still active, trying to get out the holes
where my eyes have been.

Brian Patten

Brian Patten

Little Johnny's Final Letter

Mother,
    I won't be home this evening, so
    don't worry; don't hurry to report me missing.
    Don't drain the canals to find me,
    I've decided to stay alive, don't
    search the woods, I'm not hiding,
    simply gone to get myself classified.
    Don't leave my shreddies out,
    I've done with security.
    Don't circulate my photograph to society
    I have disguised myself as a man
    and am giving priority to obscurity.
    It suits me fine;
    I have taken off my short trousers
    and put on long ones, and
    now am going out into the city, so
    don't worry; don't hurry to report me missing.

    I've rented a room without any curtains
    and sit behind the windows growing cold,
    heard your plea on the radio this morning,
    you sounded sad and strangely old. . . .

Brian Patten

A Blade of Grass

You ask for a poem.
I offer you a blade of grass.
You say it is not good enough.
You ask for a poem.

I say this blade of grass will do.
It has dressed itself in frost,
It is more immediate
Than any image of my making.

You say it is not a poem,
It is a blade of grass and grass
Is not quite good enough.
I offer you a blade of grass.

You are indignant.
You say it is too easy to offer grass.
It is absurd.
Anyone can offer a blade of grass.

You ask for a poem.
And so I write you a tragedy about
How a blade of grass
Becomes more and more difficult to offer,

And about how as you grow older
A blade of grass
Becomes more difficult to accept.

Brian Patten

Albatross Ramble

I woke this morning to find an albatross staring at me.
Funny, it wasn't there last night.
Last night I was alone.

The albatross lay on the bed.
The sheets were soaking.

I live miles from any coast.
I invited no mad sailors home.
I dreamt of no oceans.

The bird is alive, it watches me carefully.
I watch it carefully.
For some particular reason I think
Maybe we deserve one another.

It's sunny outside, spring even.
The sky is bright; it is alive.

I remember I have someone to meet,
Someone clear, someone with whom I'm calm,
Someone who lets things glow.

As I put on my overcoat to go out
I think that maybe after all
I don't deserve this bird.

Albatrosses cause hang-ups.
There's not much I can do with them.
I can't give them in to zoos.
The attendants have enough albatrosses.

Nobody is particularly eager to take it from me.

Maybe, I think, the bird's in the wrong house.
Maybe it meant to go next door.
Maybe some sailor lives next door.
Maybe it belongs to the man upstairs.
Maybe it belongs to the girls in the basement.
It must belong to someone.

I rush into the corridor and shout:
'Does anyone own an albatross? Has anyone lost it?
There's an albatross in my room!'

I'm met by an awkward silence.

I know the man upstairs is not happy.
I know the girls in the basement wander lost among the
   furniture.
Maybe they're trying to get rid of it
And won't own up.
Maybe they've palmed the albatross off on me.

I don't want an albatross; I don't want this bird;
I've got someone to meet,
Someone patient, someone good and healthy,
Someone whose hands are warm and whose grin
Makes everything babble and say yes.
I'd not like my friend to meet the albatross.

It would eat those smiles;
It would bother that patience;

It would peck at those hands
Till they turned sour and ancient.

Although I have made albatross traps,
Although I have sprayed the thing with glue,
Although I have fed it every poison available,
It still persists in living,
This bird with peculiar shadows
Casts its darkness over everything.

If I go out it would only follow.
It would flop in the seat next to me on the bus,
Scowling at the passengers.
If I took it to the park it would only bother the ducks,
Haunt couples in rowing boats,
Tell the trees it's winter.
It would be patted by policemen as they gently asked:
'Have you an albatross licence?'

Gloom bird, doom bird,
I can do nothing about it.
There are no albatross-exterminators in the directory;
I looked for hours.

Maybe it will stay with me right through summer;
Maybe it has no intentions of leaving.
I'll grow disturbed with this bird never leaving,
This alien bird with me all the time.

And now my friend is knocking on the door,
Less patient, frowning,
A bit sad and angry.

I'll sit behind this door and make noises like an albatross.
A terrible crying.
I'll put my mouth to the keyhole and wail albatross wails.
My friend will know then
I have an albatross in my room.
My friend will sympathize with me,
Go away knowing it's not my fault I can't open the door.

I'll wait here; I might devise some plan:
It's spring and everything is good but for this.

This morning I woke with an albatross in my room.
There's nothing much I can do about it until it goes away.

Brian Patten

The Arrival of the Bee Box

I ordered this, this clean wood box
Square as a chair and almost too heavy to lift.
I would say it was the coffin of a midget
Or a square baby
Were there not such a din in it.

The box is locked, it is dangerous.
I have to live with it overnight
And I can't keep away from it.
There are no windows, so I can't see what is in there.
There is only a little grid, no exit.

I put my eye to the grid.
It is dark, dark,
With the swarmy feeling of African hands
Minute and shrunk for export,
Black on black, angrily clambering.

How can I let them out?
It is the noise that appals me most of all,
The unintelligible syllables.
It is like a Roman mob,
Small, taken one by one, but my god, together!

I lay my ear to furious Latin.
I am not a Caesar.
I have simply ordered a box of maniacs.
They can be sent back.
They can die, I need feed them nothing, I am the owner.

I wonder how hungry they are.
I wonder if they would forget me

If I just undid the locks and stood back and turned into a tree.
There is the laburnum, its blond colonnades,
And the petticoats of the cherry.

They might ignore me immediately
In my moon suit and funeral veil.
I am no source of honey
So why should they turn on me?
Tomorrow I will be sweet God, I will set them free.

The box is only temporary.

Sylvia Plath

The Rabbit Catcher

It was a place of force—
The wind gagging my mouth with my own blown hair,
Tearing off my voice, and the sea
Blinding me with its lights, the lives of the dead
Unreeling in it, spreading like oil.

I tasted the malignity of the gorse,
Its black spikes,
The extreme unction of its yellow candle-flowers.
They had an efficiency, a great beauty,
And were extravagant, like torture.

There was only one place to get to.
Simmering, perfumed,
The paths narrowed into the hollow.
And the snares almost effaced themselves—
Zeroes, shutting on nothing,

Set close, like birth pangs.
The absence of shrieks
Made a hole in the hot day, a vacancy.
The glassy light was a clear wall,
The thickets quiet.

I felt a still busyness, an intent.
I felt hands round a tea mug, dull, blunt,
Ringing the white china.
How they awaited him, those little deaths!
They waited like sweethearts. They excited him.

And we, too, had a relationship—
Tight wires between us,
Pegs too deep to uproot, and a mind like a ring
Sliding shut on some quick thing,
The constriction killing me also.

Sylvia Plath

Pheasant

You said you would kill it this morning.
Do not kill it. It startles me still,
The jut of that odd, dark head, pacing

Through the uncut grass on the elm's hill.
It is something to own a pheasant,
Or just to be visited at all.

I am not mystical: it isn't
As if I thought it had a spirit.
It is simply in its element.

That gives it a kingliness, a right.
The print of its big foot last winter,
The tail-track, on the snow in our court—

The wonder of it, in that pallor,
Through crosshatch of sparrow and starling.
Is it its rareness, then? It is rare.

But a dozen would be worth having,
A hundred, on that hill—green and red,
Crossing and recrossing: a fine thing!

It is such a good shape, so vivid.
It's a little cornucopia.
It unclaps, brown as a leaf, and loud,

Settles in the elm, and is easy.
It was sunning in the narcissi.
I trespass stupidly. Let be, let be.

Sylvia Plath

All the Dead Dears

*In the Archaeological Museum in Cambridge is a
stone coffin of the fourth century A.D. containing the
skeletons of a woman, a mouse and a shrew. The
ankle-bone of the woman has been slightly gnawn.*

Rigged poker-stiff on her back
With a granite grin
This antique museum-cased lady
Lies, companioned by the gimcrack
Relics of a mouse and a shrew
That battened for a day on her ankle-bone.

These three, unmasked now, bear
Dry witness
To the gross eating game
We'd wink at if we didn't hear
Stars grinding, crumb by crumb,
Our own grist down to its bony face.

How they grip us through thin and thick,
These barnacle dead!
This lady here's no kin
Of mine, yet kin she is: she'll suck
Blood and whistle my marrow clean
To prove it. As I think now of her head,

From the mercury-backed glass
Mother, grandmother, greatgrandmother
Reach hag hands to haul me in,

And an image looms under the fishpond surface
Where the daft father went down
With orange duck-feet winnowing his hair—

All the long gone darlings: they
Get back, though, soon,
Soon: be it by wakes, weddings,
Childbirths or a family barbecue:
Any touch, taste, tang's
Fit for those outlaws to ride home on,

And to sanctuary: usurping the armchair
Between tick
And tack of the clock, until we go,
Each skulled-and-crossboned Gulliver
Riddled with ghosts, to lie
Deadlocked with them, taking root as cradles rock.

Sylvia Plath

The Goring

Arena dust rusted by four bulls' blood to a dull redness,
The afternoon at a bad end under the crowd's truculence,
The ritual death each time botched among dropped capes, ill-
    judged stabs,
The strongest will seemed a will towards ceremony. Obese,
    dark-
Faced in his rich yellows, tassels, pompons, braid, the picador

Rode out against the fifth bull to brace his pike and slowly bear
Down deep into the bent bull-neck. Cumbrous routine, not
    artwork.
Instinct for art began with the bull's horn lofting in the mob's
Hush a lumped man-shape. The whole act formal, fluent as a
    dance.
Blood faultlessly broached redeemed the sullied air, the earth's
    grossness.

Sylvia Plath

Old Ladies' Home

Sharded in black, like beetles,
Frail as antique earthenware
One breath might shiver to bits,
The old women creep out here
To sun on the rocks or prop
Themselves up against the wall
Whose stones keep a little heat.

Needles knit in a bird-beaked
Counterpoint to their voices:
Sons, daughters, daughters and sons,
Distant and cold as photos,
Grandchildren nobody knows.
Age wears the best black fabric
Rust-red or green as lichens,

At owl-call the old ghosts flock
To hustle them off the lawn.
From beds boxed-in like coffins
The bonneted ladies grin.
And Death, that bald-head buzzard,
Stalls in halls where the lamp wick
Shortens with each breath drawn.

Sylvia Plath

Thirteen Ways of Looking at a Blackboard

I

The blackboard is clean.
The master must be coming.

II

The vigilant mosquito bites on a rising pitch.
The chalk bristles over the blackboard.

III

Among twenty silent children
The only moving thing
Is the chalk's white finger.

IV

O young white cricketers,
Aching for the greensward,
Do you not see how my moving hand
Whitens the black board?

V

A man and a child
Are one.
A man and a child and a blackboard
Are three.

VI

Some wield their sticks of chalk
Like torches in dark rooms.
I make up my blackboard
Like the face of an actor.

VII

I was of three minds
Like a room
In which there are three blackboards.

VIII

I dream.
I am an albino.

IX

I wake.
I forget a word.
The chalk snaps on the blackboard.

X

Twenty silent children
Staring at the blackboard.
On one wall of each of twenty nurseries
The light has gone out.

XI

He ambles among the white rocks of Dover,
Crushing pebbles with black boots.
He is a small blackboard
Writing on chalk.

XII

It is the Christmas holidays.
The white snow lies in the long black branches.
The black board
In the silent schoolroom
Perches on two stubby branches.

XIII

The flesh that is white
Wastes over the bones that are chalk,
Both in the day
And through the black night.

Peter Redgrove

At the Edge of the Wood

First, boys out of school went out of their way home
To detonate the windows; at each smash
Piping with delight and skipping with fright
Of a ghost of the old man popping over his hedge,
Shrieking and nodding from the gate.
Then the game palled, since it was only breaking the
    silence.
The rain sluiced through the starred gaps,
Crept up walls and into the brick; frost bit and
    munched;
Weeds craned in and leant on the doors.
Now it is a plot without trees let into the wood
Piled high with tangle and tousle
Buried parapets and roots picking at the last mortar
Though the chimney still stands sheathed in leaves
And you can see for the time being where in a nook
A briony burst its pot with a shower of roots
And back through the press of shrubs and stems
Deep-coils into the woods.

Peter Redgrove

A Storm

Somebody is throttling that tree
By the way it's threshing about;
I'm glad it's no one I know, or me,
The head thrust back at the throat,

Green hair tumbled and cracking throat.
His thumbs drive into her windpipe,
She cannot cry out,
Only swishing and groaning: death swells ripe,

The light is dimming but the fight goes on.
Chips strike my window. In the morning, there
Stands the tree, still, bushy and calm,
Not as I saw it, twisted heel to ear,

But fluffed up, boughs chafing slightly.
What's become of her attacker?
I'm glad he's not mine or known to me,
Flipped to the ground, heel over ear:

She preens herself, with a soft bough-purr.
Was he swallowed up, lip over ear?
He's gone anyway. The path is thick in her fur.
Am I a friend, may I walk near?

Peter Redgrove

Design

The designer sits, head in hand.
What costume could be better for battle, the more sensible?
Why, one blood won't mar.
I'll score it with scarlet.

But often men outlast deep wounds.
Some blood is old, and black.
Let's have a tatter, then, I slash scarlet black.

And here is a master-stroke. Let it be random tatter.
Random tables fed into the looms.
Thus as they advance none perhaps are wounded,

Or all are, mortally, and ripped from the field.
Horrible half-dry men.
Yes. Let them advance as though ripped from the clay.
One of the many patterns of battle.
And pipeclay features with blacking sockets, General.

Peter Redgrove

Gentlemen

We fight, I'm afraid, bite and scratch,
Gentlemen, in our work,
Or meditate, over the lighted match,
The horseman and the flaming brand,
Gentlemen riding to town.

It is a pity, I say, there are so many of us
Stiffly packed in our seats,
A little thinning would not come amiss,
Gentlemen riding to work.

The easy dispersal of ashes—then
O Lord I could pray
For that puff of dirt that nudges me,
Gentlemen riding to town.

Stiff collar, bowler, gloves and
Black tie,
Grey and severe, and in my hand
The salt cambric crumpled away,
Gentlemen riding to work,
Ah, then I should walk for a time alone
Grizzle with fine dignity,
Tender respect when I got back
Unjostled next day in town,
Gentlemen! colleagues!
Unjostled next day at work.

Gentlemen riding to work
Eagerly looking around to choke
Back real grief, real tears,
Looking around as the tube-train stops
For the prosperous figure best fitted for corpse
And, how sad is death, how very sad.

Peter Redgrove

Who's Your Daddy?

(Ans.: 'H.M.S. Ark Royal!'—wartime joke)

I see a great battleship moored in the snow
I see the silvery pencils of guns that bristle
I remake this image, I try to,
It is a pine cone of lunar metal
Doors hinge in its steel, flakes fly,
Warm glows emerge
I see pollen
I see a pine cone consecrated to Attis
I see an ark
I know there are scrolls
Containing royal mysteries inside

Called explosives
Causing mysterious deaths understood by computer
It is a battleship
This will not be countermanded
It is a great battleship moored in the snow

It is not a white spider
Flying in its cracked web of the lake

It is not the discarded surplice
Of the summer-god, still warm inside

It is a battleship containing sailors
Trained to navigate and kill

It is no wedding-gown
Or wedding blouse with golden buttons
From which light shines across snowy sheets
It is no iced honey-cake of the sacrament of
    marriage
In which the honey is sweet light
That will last a couple of years
Of married breakfasts

It is a battleship

Commanded
Metal commanded
By a man with steel-ringed eyes
By a man with golden wedded cuffs
Under orders

It is no felled yule-log
Stuffed with presents
The honey-log of a sedated bear

It awaits orders understood by computer

It is the sledge made of dead men's nails,
The glittering horse of scythes,
The refrigerator of snowy carcases.

Peter Redgrove

Girls and the Rain

Between one sentence
and the next,
between one poem
and its sister,
my room has grown dark
It's nearly noon
but the sky is blueblack,
a splashboard for the rain
that is at last falling,
healing the wounds of girls
who are rescued by the rain
from a sad deformed morning

Waiting for rain,
my body was awkward
as the dusty cluttered furniture

and my empty purse
gaped open on the table

For me
and for the seaside girls like me,
the rainstorm
with its drops bevelling the windows,
the stammer and hiss of hail,
the revelation of the weather's veil,
the underside of the sky soaking
and clinging to the trees:
this is what we need

Dark icy tears fall from the sky
God, like a pale park-keeper, weeps for us,
tears tasting of piano-keyboards

And we are happier in our dark houses,
we draw our chairs close to the window
and peer through the glass at ourselves
seen as cloud-women
weeping ourselves clean

We dance in the last of the drizzle

Penelope Shuttle

Granite Valentine
for Peter

We are sheltered
We are in our granite tent
pitched two hundred years ago
and still baffling the winters
Against the night windows
Cornish snow is guzzling the wind
The snowflakes melt,
the lawns are hot-blooded here,
The wind butts at the doors,
whines along the cobweb passages

I sit by the fire,
on my lap is the book
you gave me this morning
'Granite Crosses of West Cornwall'

I open the book and read
'an ancient cross in the middle
of a field at Wicca'

This is the first Valentine
I've written
It came out of the gusty guesswork
of the spring
and commemorates one day
in our interwoven calendar

Penelope Shuttle

Autumn

Autumn sharpens all sense
With the twin blades of coal and frost.
Fog in the street hides misty hollows:
Incense of fireworks and mud.
Bayrose and blackberries wilt
Where stinging-nettles weep and rot.

I dreamed of Salt Peter walking
(Seawrack clinging to his lips)
Through the mist lit by a rosebay sun:
Jack Frost came in time to help him cure
The autumn pig
And puzzle out the year's hard lock.
They tilted up the winter-mill
Churning snow which burned like sulphur.

Lamp posts glitter through fog:
Sulphur-torches on a road
That has no turning—
Except backwards.

II

I laced up my autumn boots,
Put on a coat and stalked from lamp to lamp
Where darkness was lighter than the home
With shouts of my own people:
Stray dogs and bonfires flicker,
Cats flee along secret by-paths
Of curved teeth.

Frost painted my cheeks with marble cold
And my toes with luminous tips
In their hide-outs:
But none of us kids liked rain
Drizzling on moss and bricks,

Found the house more homely
For the shelter and the food we got—
Brothers and sisters going through one
Door for warmth.

The cold ambushed us when we got to bed
All four between brass nobs and rails,
An attic to ourselves in a minute cottage
In the Valley of the Leen where Nottingham
Stopped on its outward march,
Fixed by the green fields.

Two in the middle were warmest:
Except for suffocation, bliss.
But those on the outside
One of whom was me
Slept with a grip of bedclothes
In their fists, a fight kept up
Throughout grey dreams of Jack Frost
And Salt Peter when
To let go or relax
Meant shivering the whole long dawn.

III

That's winter
But autumn led to it
And into spring which marched
Again to autumn. Time is a wheel
And I stand in the middle
Facing one way, the roundabout
That spins each season slowly in
And either warms my face or freezes it.

Time lives nowhere but in memory,
Keeps me warm against the frost
And cool from the sun's bleak fire.

Alan Sillitoe

Alchemist

Lead melts. If I saw lead, I melted it,
Poured it into sand and made shapes.
I melted all I'd got, even my own, eventually.

I watched that lead soldier's rifle wilt
In an old tin-can on a gas flame
Caught like a straw going down
From an invisible spark of summer.
He stood to attention in the tin
Rim gripped by fanatic pliers
That believed in life and nothing else—
From the old man's tool-kit
Looked on by beady scientific eyes
That vandalised a leaden grenadier.

The head sagged, sweating under a greater
Heat than Waterloo or Alma.
With tired feet he leaned against the side
And lost an arm where no black grapeshot came.
His useless knees gave way,
A pool half spreading to his once proud groin,
Waist and busby falling in, as sentry-go
At such an India became too hard,
And he lay down without pillow or blanket
Never to get up and see home again.

Another one. Two more. I threw them in
And these went quicker, an elegant patrol
Dissolving in that infernal pit.
My eyes watered from the heat and fumes of painted
Soldiers melting under their own smoke,
The fire with me, hands hard at the plier-grip
Eyes cool but squinting
At these soldiers rendered
To a patch of peaceful lead
At the bottom of a tin.

Swords into ploughshares:
With the gas turned off I wondered
What to do with so much marvellous
Dead lead that hardened
As I looked, and looked,
And looked at it.

Alan Sillitoe

The River has Burst
its Banks

The river has burst its banks
All cathedrals sliding away
Blue cloud pulling at each spire
Hillocks shoving from behind. . . .

Those several channels now are one wide lake
That wide and leisurely meandering is gone
You cannot shout from one side to the other—
You try to swim and get dragged out to sea.

There was no rain to swell the river
Nor any fissure shot it from below
But that slow river is now fledged and roaring
Collapsing all its banks and spreading wide.

The spire and nave and transept crumble in
The branches of a tree catch on it to be saved:
Children laugh and crayon in another sun
To join the other six and dry this river up

This forceput monster eating at the land
Where tree and spire sink back to the fishes:
Every shore is melting fast
From that unholy water pulling villages and cities in.

Alan Sillitoe

The Friday Fish

For Percy Jarrett

We lived ramshackle that summer in a cabin
toppling onto the shore; a big madrona,
red-skinned, smooth-limbed, curved the stiff horizon
that exchanged our gaze through age-smeared windows;
the nearby headland held in clumsy brush
the cabins and wrecked cars of the Reservation.

It was Friday. We'd let the dinghy lie
awash all week to swell the planks. The tide
had drowned the barnacled rocks, the spitting clam-bed,
and wriggled at the shingle. We dragged her down,
keel rasping pebbles, pushed her off, and jumped.
Our tackle rattled. We would jig for cod.

Smoke rose in grey ropes from the Reservation
where nobody moved; the water slid,
unwrinkling, dark; the sun blurred, faltered, bloomed
soft crimson; the horizon smeared with blood.
But we were in the shadow of the land,
and only our faces altered, flushed and carved
by patience and the sun's death. Up and down
the tips of our rods moved—then something bit:
you struck, reeled in; the trace was bitten through.

That was the way it went for perhaps an hour.
Figures came out of the cabin, waved their questions
under the madrona. Children cried
excitements of expectation thin as loss.
But all the traces broke. The sea grew darker.
The sky was flushed. Winds chilled us from the West.

A wire trace, I said. *We'll fix the bastards!*
A wire trace it was: we gently knocked
our leads upon the bottom, reeled in some inches,
lifted, and let fall, kept patient rhythm,
gazing off at lengthening swallowing shadows.
Most of the Reservation had turned black.

And then it bit. I struck, reeled in. At first
it was a dream in the water, a swerve of meaning
greenly transient, then a slap and flash
of exclamation at the side of the boat,
diving, dragging down, then back, then up
slowly to suddenly kick. Too late. The net
scooped up: it thrashed between our drowning feet.
I took the club and killed. Once. Twice. Again.
The sky was watery blood. I split the skull.

Rowing back, the questions came over the water.
'Dogfish—three foot, maybe!' 'Dogfish?' 'Yes.'
Stubborn to gain from murder, I refused
distaste and doubt, upon the beached log laid
the long corpse out, picked up the knife, and at
the first brush of the blade it curved and jerked
in jacknife, and its jaw snapped, plap! You dropped
the rag. *'It's dead,'* I said. *'Just nerves. Don't fret.'*
'Dead?' you said. *'Quite dead!'* The knife was not
half sharp enough; the wet skin rasped our hands;
the scales were chips of mica, splinter-thin;
but, heaving from the elbow, I at last
ripped up the belly, and the spill of gut
slopped out in red and silver blotched with black,
looped, sagged, and squirming. Using both my hands
I grappled it, and threw. You turned aside
uneasily. Then, three yards out to sea,
we saw the stomach sac, still round, float up
and in its glistening five small black fish
still blindly swimming, prisoners.
                                        'They're alive!'
You said. We could not move. The slippery knife
was rigid in my hand. And *'Let them out!'*
you cried, too late.
                        The tide was black. The waves
bore them into the vast unravelling dark
we shuddered at, as, heaving up our catch,
we climbed the track beneath the black madrona,

turning at the top, horizon gone,
the Reservation fathomless in gloom.

Robin Skelton

John Arthur

John Arthur walks the tideline-scribbled sand,
having nothing else to do but let things slide,
driftwood, wreckage, weed kicked into mounds,
poked and prodded, taffled and let bide.

You'd think, his tar-smeared rain-stained mac
flapping at every slouched lunge of the knee,
he had a wisdom that we strangers lack,
some slow-tongued gnomon of sand, wind, and sea,

and was content. You'd think that if you could,
unwilling to believe him derelict,
walking beside great waters whose brown flood
roars down a wreckers' harvest to be picked—

kindling (of course) its staple, but much more
washed from the fat black coasters as they roll—
you'd figure him an uncrowned ignorant Lear
trapped on the blustered edges of the world,

and you'd be wrong all through, because John Arthur
has nothing else to do but let things slide;
driftwood and sunlight, weed and wanting, slither
endlessly through him like the sour brown tide,

and days are just for filling in with time.
Get closer and you'll see his sandblind stare.
One foot drags, one hand twitches, waves crash down
and mile and mile on mile destroy the shore.

Robin Skelton

Ballad of Billy Barker

A gay young widow woman
with eyes as green as glass
and a bandy-legged prospector
with slum upon his ass;
you split your sides to think of it,
but I lie stiff as stone:
it's curtains now for English Bill
in Victoria Old Men's Home.

On Williams Creek in August
back in sixty two
the claims ran dry. The black sand let
no speck of colour through.
Ned Stout came down the canyon
and found his gulch and struck;
I followed him, staked out my claim,
and drove down through the rock.

Jumped ship, I did, and followed up
the blinding yellow dream.
The Fraser lashed its rolling stones
till mud was silver cream;
the walls of Hell's Gate cliffed me in
and Jackass Mountain shook
its dirt-brown back in mockery as
I trailed to stake my luck.

Seven of us worked that shaft.
The sun danced with the heat.
Ten feet we went and nothing showed.
Ten feet and then ten feet.
At thirty feet the cloud came up;
the sky was solid lead;
the windlass juddered at each hoist;
the wind sobbed for the dead.

Seven of us choked for breath.
I went down in the pit.
At forty feet the rain came down;

we took another foot.
A crazy sailor and six men
hauled rope till they were blind;
at fifty feet no colours showed
and even hope was mined.

Hope, Faith, Prayer were all mined out
and rubble piled up high
around the shaft-house hacked out from
the pines that hacked the sky;
mud welled; rain swaled; ropes cut and slid,
and heart and mouth were dry.

At sea the waters curve away
green satin from the bow,
and foam as thick as milk swirls out
along the track we plough,
and waves heave tall as hills and fall
like hills upon the deck.
The hills that stood round Williams Creek
would neither bend nor break.

The hills that frowned their forest black
above our hunch and sweat
rocked no horizons for our eyes,
nor shone out in the night
with greens and blues and grains of gold
as I've seen on the sea.
We took another foot. The dream
stood shuddering over me.

The yellow dream, the blinding dream
I'd taken for my life
stood over me. I felt its breath.
Its eyes cut like a knife.
I took another foot. Time stopped.
I heard it end my life.

I heard it finish, and I struck.
Five dollars to the pan;
and seven men on Williams Creek

went crazy to a man.
A thousand dollars every foot
we took out from that clay
and seven men on Williams Creek
were blinded by the day.

Drinks we had. Three days we drank
and all on English Bill.
I think I drank a thousand lives
at every swig and spill,
a thousand miners trailing north,
a thousand narrow pits
upon the benches by the creeks
where golden bones would sit.

I think in every glass I saw
a face and then a face;
a woman with long yellow hair
leaned into my embrace,
a widow with eyes green as grass
and lips as red as blood,
but at her back another face
as black as the wet wood.

Another face as black as wood,
with skin as soft as slum
and eyes as blind as pebbled quartz,
and gaping mouth as dumb
as Blessing's mouth, or Barry's mouth
that opened as he swung.

I met her in Victoria by
the bitter chilling strait;
some traded skins; I traded gold
and traded for a mate,
a London widow woman
and her golden hair and luck:
I took her up the Fraser
through the roaring mocking rock.

I took her up to Barkerville;
I should have let her be.
The gold ran out; the claim ran dry;
she ran loose as the sea;
her greens of satin, foams of silk
heaved up to prow on prow:
the sea's a wicked smother, but
I know a worse one now.

The sea's a wicked country;
its green hills lift and drown:
but earth's a played-out working
when you've thrown your money down.
I worked as cook; I begged; I washed;
my pans were grey with stone:
it's curtains now for English Bill
in Victoria Old Men's Home.

It's headstones now for English Bill.
My drinking roaring mouth
burns cancer where her kisses burned
and has a graver drouth,
and as I gape I see her face,
but then that other face
that looked on me in Williams Creek
and rotted like the race—

the race of men that dragged their packs
up canyons to the creek,
the race that heard my pick crack down
into that yellow strike,
whose deaths built law and church and state
upon my broken stone,
But Billy Barker's dead and gone
in Victoria Old Men's Home.

Robin Skelton

The Pity

I cut my hands on the cords at the strangling post, but no blood spilled from my veins, instead of blood I watched and saw the pity run out of me   *MAO TSE-TUNG*

She was destroyed, and my child ceased in her belly.
In Kiang-si we had walked in the clear morning,
she hanging back, barefoot, childbig. Crossing
the plank bridge I saw the falling mountain
with its stream hang still. The land lay like a bowl
of pebbles, hills behind me at its rim. A hawk
splayed in the wind, dived to kill; so sparrows die.
China was patience you said: the sketched lines
of valley, of the reaching twig, all still, rest in motion;
a large pale flower twitching, a flower waiting, open.
So a vast land itched for death, its people mild
and ministered.
                    But the cockroach and the grinning toad
drawn beautiful was China; the fly grown fat on flesh,
glittering in heat. I was lashed and drained
of the gentle passion. Patience was prised from me.
I picked lice from my hair. You thought me gentle still.
I ate filth, wore it, would have died in filth.

The horned and hanging bat sees a bat's world.
Fish quiver in the shallows, cold as their element,
thinking water. I wore contempt, grew hatred.
I was locked and jailed. She that was my wife
was garrotted. And compassion had not anything to do
with this; she was destroyed where I could hear,
and the child ceased in her.

Compassion cannot go forever in the sun,
paraded, bowing, twig-like. It rests,
and somewhere takes the hawk's wing, diving.
She was destroyed and my child ceased.
I cut my hands on the cords at the strangling post,
but no blood spilled from my veins;
instead of blood I watched and saw the pity run out of me.

Ken Smith

The Hunter

On the hill three hawks
on spread feathers
fish the summer grass

In summer on the bare hill
the light falls in sheets

The sheep turn like ships
at their moorings

The crows fly downwind
their sounds fall from the sky
downwind they are crying

Man, dog, birds. On the hill
sheep and the wrenched grass
lies downwind. It is summer

The birds crossing the sky
are naked, the light falls
downwind they are falling

It is summer
dog and man share the hill
sniff the air
hunt the bird

As we look in the tunnel
for the end
for the bleak
unblinking eye of the daylight

he is looking
for the black holes in the sky

Ken Smith

Spring Poem

Leaves pierce upward
between stones
drop grits of dead soil
their pulp bodies fatten

the blades of the snowdrop
fencing the flower's mouth
are emerald
repeating

Many colours fasten
as spring hardens—
gorse and daffodil start up like snow
and the crocus lifts up
its teeth
in impending grasses

there is green on the earth
the grass snow turned black
puts up fingers
whose groping
under the frost-withered stems
puts them aside

the petals
keep coming back
each time spring says things do not die
many lives most underground
strain to the first spray of rain
flicker
above grass
the filler of spaces
that will not be still
it lifts and it bends
it is sure in its gesture
the colours run out

the shadows of March leaves
falling
to meet them
bear down the grass

Ken Smith

A description of the Lichway or corpse-road across Dartmoor

Lich: Old English *lic* as a suffix for -like (likely).
Used also as a noun, a word for form, body, or
corpse: the substance of a thing. Note also the
Anglo-Saxon *hlinc* whose nearest synonym is
ridge, hence a word by transfer for boundary, or a
path cresting a ridge, so a word for link.

From Babeny and Pizwell
west to Lydford 11½ miles
as the crow flies who needs
carry only his own death

It seems not much,
by their ways a day and a half-day's
travel got the corpse
to Lydford Church, setting

the dead down again.
Hardly a tree for shade,
none for coffinwood. In rain
the moor runs like a sieve,

the brooks flood, clay pulls
to the roll of the slope.
In what boots they went
is not said, nor their curses

By 1260 these villages
let off that passage.

The rest, scattered farms, inns,
Merripits and Bellever

trudged on, the Forest's dead
on the dead's road converged
across Longaford, the Cowsic,
under Whittor and Whittaburrow

The king's land, men struggled
away from their masters,
scratching for tin, thin
scrawny cattle, a few oats

shared with the beasts
under one roof, chaff blown
in the Atlantic wind, survived
by the rain and fern

And gone. Their hands
lifted the stone, sifted
the streams for metal. In winter
salted the dead down

Not long back a traveller
lifted the bench lid on a corpse
floating in brine—the innkeeper
saved for spring burial

Cut by enclosures, mines,
artillery ranges, theirs
is the dead's print, pressing
of feet through a strange land

Ken Smith

The Wild Dog

[handwritten: regular Rhyme.]

The City Dog goes to the drinking trough, *[handwritten: a]*
He waves his tail and laughs, and goes when he has had
     enough *[handwritten: a]*
His intelligence is on the brink *[handwritten: b]*
Of human intelligence. He knows the Council will give him *[handwritten: 1]*
     a drink. *[handwritten: b]*

[handwritten right margin: Different 2 Line Lengths.]

The Wild Dog is not such an animal,
Untouched by human kind, he is inimical,
He keeps his tail stiff, his eyes blink,
And he goes to the river when he wants a drink.
He goes to the river, he stamps on the mud, *[handwritten: b]*
And at night he sleeps in the dark wood. *[handwritten: b.]*

Stevie Smith

Not Waving but Drowning

Nobody heard him, the dead man, *[handwritten: a]*
But still he lay moaning: *[handwritten: b]*
I was much further out than you thought *[handwritten: c]*
And not waving but drowning. *[handwritten: b]*

[handwritten right margin: no jaunty regular rhyming scheme.]

Poor chap, he always loved larking
And now he's dead
It must have been too cold for him his heart
     gave way,
They said.

Oh, no no no, it was too cold always
(Still the dead one lay moaning)
I was much too far out all my life
And not waving but drowning.

Stevie Smith

Widowhood
or The Home-Coming of Lady Ross
(Her husband, the Lord of the Isles, is dead, and
she lives alone by the sea)

Nobody hears me, nobody sees me,
My father, the General, used to say
He had only to come into a room
For everybody else to go out of it.

('Ach, wie schrecklich, so alt zu sein,
    Und diese schrecklichen Tränensäcke,
    Als wenn sie viel geweint hätte!'
Said the young girl to her friend,
In the hotel at Baden.)

My heart is a frozen lump,
I look forward to nothing but Death,
I am glad Harold is not here
To see me now.

('Oh how awful, to be so old,
    And those awful tear-tracks on her cheeks,
    As if she had cried a lot!'
Said the young girl to her friend
In the hotel at Cheltenham.)

Harold loved the hotel at Baden and the hotel at Cheltenham
He loved staying in hotels, he loved staying in 'em.

Now I live alone by the sea
And I am happy as never I used to be,
Harold, can you forgive me?
My family were never much good in company.

That's what you used to say, dear, do you remember, when I
    stayed in my room
In the hotel at Baden, or wherever it might be, Up you would
    come
Rushing, and kiss me and cry: Rhoda, your family,
I must say, are not much good in company.

Oh Harold, our house looks so beautiful today,
Why did you always want to go away?

Stevie Smith

Croft

Aloft,
In the loft,
Sits Croft;
He is soft.

Stevie Smith

The Jungle Husband

Dearest Evelyn, I often think of you
Out with the guns in the jungle stew
Yesterday I hittapotamus
I put the measurements down for you but they got lost in
    the fuss
It's not a good thing to drink out here
You know, I've practically given it up dear.
Tomorrow I am going alone a long way
Into the jungle. It is all grey
But green on top
Only sometimes when a tree has fallen
The sun comes down plop, it is quite appalling.
You never want to go in a jungle pool
In the hot sun, it would be the act of a fool
Because it's always full of anacondas, Evelyn, not looking
    ill-fed
I'll say. So no more now, from your loving husband,
    Wilfred.

Stevie Smith

[handwritten annotations: it rhymes but untidy + strained like a child's poetry. ludicrous on surface but pathetic underneath. funny poem. comic + odd.]

Traveling Through the Dark

Traveling through the dark I found a deer
dead on the edge of the Wilson River road.
It is usually best to roll them into the canyon:
that road is narrow; to swerve might make more dead.

By glow of the tail-light I stumbled back of the car
and stood by the heap, a doe, a recent killing;
she had stiffened already, almost cold.
I dragged her off; she was large in the belly.

My fingers touching her side brought me the reason—
her side was warm; her fawn lay there waiting,
alive, still, never to be born.
Beside that mountain road I hesitated.

The car aimed ahead its lowered parking lights;
under the hood purred the steady engine.
I stood in the glare of the warm exhaust turning red;
around our group I could hear the wilderness listen.

I thought hard for us all—my only swerving—,
then pushed her over the edge into the river.

William Stafford

Montana Eclogue

I

After the fall drive, the last
horseman humps down the trail south;
High Valley turns into a remote, still cathedral.
Stone Creek in its low bank turns calmly
through the trampled meadow. The one scouting
thunderhead above Long Top hangs to watch,
ready for its reinforcement due in October.

Logue, the man who always closes down the camp,
is left all alone at Clear Lake, where
he is leisurely but busy, pausing to glance across
the water toward Winter Peak. The bunkhouse
will be boarded up, the cookshack barricaded
against bears, the corral gates lashed shut.
Whatever winter needs, it will have to find
for itself, all the slow months the wind owns.

From that shore below the mountain the water
darkens; the whole surface of the lake livens,
and, upward, high miles of pine tops bend where a storm
walks the country. Deeper and deeper, autumn
floods in. Nothing can hold against that current
the aspens feel. And Logue, by being there, suddenly
carries for us everything that we can load on him,
we who have stopped indoors and let our faces
forget how storms come: that lonely man works for us.

II

Far from where we are, air owns those ranches
our trees hardly hear of, open places
braced against cold hills. Mornings, that
news hits the leaves like rain, and we
stop everything time brings, and freeze that one,
open, great, real thing—the world's gift: day.

Up there, air like an axe chops, near timberline,
the clear-cut miles the marmots own. We
try to know, all deep, all sharp, even while
busy here, that other: gripped in a job,
aimed steady at a page, or riffled by distractions,
we break free into that world of the farthest coat—air

We glimpse that last storm when the wolves
get the mountains back, when our homes will flicker
bright, then dull, then old; and the trees
will advance, knuckling their roots or lying in
windrows to match the years. We glimpse
a crack that begins to run down the wall,

and like a blanket over the window at night
that world is with us and those wolves are here.

III

Up there, ready to be part of what comes, the high lakes
lie in their magnificent beds; but men,
great as their heroes are, live by their deeds
only as a pin of shadow in a cavern their thought
gets lost in. We pause; we stand where
we are meant to be, waver as foolish as
we are, tell our lies with all the beautiful grace
an animal has when it runs—

Citizen, step back from the fire and let night
have your head: suddenly you more than hear
what is true so abruptly that God is cold:—
winter is here. What no one saw, has
come. Then everything the sun approved could
really fail? Shed from your back, the years
fall one by one, and nothing that comes
will be your fault. You breathe a few breaths
free at the thought: things can come so great
that your part is too small to count,
if winter can come.

Logue brings us all that. Earth took
the old saints, who battered their hearts,
met arrows, or died by the germs God sent;
but Logue, by being alone and occurring to us,
carries us forward a little,
and on his way out for the year will
stand by the shore and see winter in,
the great, repeated lesson every year.

A storm bends by that shore and
one flake at a time teaches grace,
even to stone.

William Stafford

Ice-Fishing

Not thinking other than how the hand works
I wait until dark here on the cold
world rind, ice-curved over simplest rock,
where the tugged river flows over hidden
springs too insidious to be quite forgotten.

When the night comes I plunge my hand
where the string of fish know their share
of the minimum. Then, bringing back my hand
is a great sunburst event; and slow
home with me over unmarked snow

In the wild flipping warmth of won-back thought
my boots, my hat, my body go.

William Stafford

In the Old Days

The wide field that was the rest of the world
came forward at evening, lowered
beyond our window shades; and Mother
spoke from her corner, about the wide field:

How someone whose eyes held another century
brought shadows of strange animals
over the mountains, and they were tethered
at night in little groups in the wide field,

And their eyes like wandering sparks
made constellations against the trees;
and how, many skies later, my father left
those animals and brought Mother news of the wide field.

Some time, some sunset, our window, she said,
would find itself again with a line of shadows
and the strange call would surround our house
and carry us away through the wide field.

Then Mother sang. But we listened, beyond:
we knew that the night she had put into a story was real.

William Stafford

They Say

Now and then in some sound you discover
a different country. Once in a barn
open and empty my guitar jumped
in my hand. Often I went back hunting
what happened, but it was always gone.

When we came down through Canada
playing at stampedes in Chilko, and Babine,
and Charlie Lake, there came a time—the drum
and the weather just so. But in Peace River
it changed and never got that way again.

But there's a country beyond all of those, to be
found and then lost. You cross borders toward home,
smuggling a whole state legally, glancing
aside at the wind or the patrol. They want you
to have it. They say, 'Song?' and they let it come.

William Stafford

On the Farm

There was Dai Puw. He was no good.
They put him in the fields to dock swedes,
And took the knife from him, when he came home
At late evening with a grin
Like the slash of a knife on his face.   Simile.

Thomas gives us a sense of place and its people. On the farm has lilting rhymes of speech

R. S. Thomas

There was Llew Puw, and he was no good.
Every evening after the ploughing
With the big tractor he would sit in his chair,
And stare into the tangled fire garden,
Opening his slow lips like a snail. *simile*

There was Huw Puw, too. What shall I say?
I have heard him whistling in the hedges
On and on, as though winter
Would never again leave those fields, *suggests bleakness...*
And all the trees were deformed. *deformity*

And lastly there was the girl:
Beauty under some spell of the beast.
Her pale face was the lantern *metaphor.*
By which they read in life's dark book
The shrill sentence: God is love.

R. S. Thomas

The girl's beauty brings them close to God in an otherwise harsh + narrow life.

Lore

Job Davies, eighty-five *jaunty lives.*
Winters old, and still alive *tough old man.*
After the slow poison *his recipe for a*
And treachery of the seasons. *long happy life,*

Miserable? Kick my arse!
It needs more than the rain's hearse, *is stay close*
Wind-drawn, to pull me off *to nature +*
The great perch of my laugh. *natural things.*

What's living but courage?
Paunch full of hot porridge,
Nerves strengthened with tea,
Peat-black, dawn found me

Mowing where the grass grew,
Bearded with golden dew.

Rhythm of the long scythe
Kept this tall frame lithe.

What to do? Stay green.
Never mind the machine,
Whose fuel is human souls.
Live large, man, and dream small.

R. S. Thomas

The Moor

[handwritten: evokes feelings]

It was like a church to me.
I entered it on soft foot, *[handwritten: — soft ground.]*
Breath held like a cap in the hand.
It was quiet.
What God was there made himself felt, *[handwritten: feel God]*
Not listened to, in clean colours *[handwritten: — communion.]*
That brought a moistening of the eye, *[handwritten: emotional]*
In movement of the wind over grass.

There were no prayers said. But stillness
Of the heart's passions—that was praise
Enough; and the mind's cession *[handwritten: close to god]*
Of its kingdom. I walked on, *[handwritten: opening heart.]*
Simple and poor, while the air crumbled
And broke on me generously as bread.

R. S. Thomas

Ravens

[handwritten: Romantic + mythical]

It was the time of the election.
The ravens loitered above the hill
In slow circles; they had all air
To themselves. No eyes were lifted

From the streets, no ears heard
Them exulting, recalling their long
History, presidents of the battles
Of flesh, the sly connoisseurs   *alliteration*
Of carrion; desultory flags
Of darkness, saddening the sky
At Catraeth and further back,
When two, who should have been friends,   *fight over woman*
Contended in the innocent light
For the woman in her downpour of hair.

fits in with mood of poem.

R. S. Thomas

Waiting with the Snowy Owls

Their yellow eyes as blank as the end   *impression. bleak winter*
Of winter under the chickenwire,
Nine snowy owls are waiting.

They stand on the ground and stare at anything   *no hope of freedom.*
Moving, their leg-tufts drifting
Like snow over their talons.

They came south like the snow, when winter hardened
Behind them, to be met by the shots and shouts
Of all our finders and keepers.

Now they wait under the sun for it to melt
What holds them, to run from them or stir
The thawed halves of hearts at their feet.

They stare through the mesh at the green welter
Of spring in the children's zoo. I wait.
On the walk beside them, unable to read or write.   *fascinated.*

David Wagoner

David Wagoner

Trying to Think by a Steel Mill

Facing this heavy industry, I try to name the substance
Of what's between us: the barbed wire crowning the gate
Was drawn from the heart of pig iron; men pass through
    smoke,
Smoking, in sheets of steel they pay for and pay for,
Toward blast furnaces and coke ovens, toward alloys boiling
Red and blue in the open hearth, to the jagged scrap heap.

Suddenly, it strikes me like a part flying out of a machine.
It hits me hard, like something I've heard shouted
To straighten me out: thinking is brittle as cast-iron.
You must cram oxygen through it to burn the impurities,
Then heap it downwind, smoke-stack it up and around
Till it falls on houses and trees in a corrosive dust,

But the trouble with thinking then is it won't stay home,
It walks around and stares at the gray case-hardened rivers,
It won't stay in school or in jail or the hospital, and it won't
Work, and it doesn't look or act like thinking:
It's strictly functional like drop-forged hardware,
But oxygen, breath by breath, comes rusting back at it.

David Wagoner

Talking Back

This green-and-red, yellow-naped Amazon parrot, Pythagoras,
Is the master of our kitchen table. *Every good boy*
Does fine! he shouts, hanging upside down, and *Pieces of eight*
And gold doubloons! in his cage whose latches he picked with ease
Till we bought a padlock, *To market, to market, to buy a fat pig*!
Home again, home again, and he rings his brass bell, as militant
As salvation, or knocks his trapeze like a punching bag with his
    beak

Or outfakes and ripostes the treacherous cluster of measuring
     spoons
Which he pretends are out for his blood. How many times
Have I wished him back in his jungle? Instead, he brings it here
Daily with a voice like sawgrass in raucous counterpoint
To after-work traffic, washing machines, or electric razors
As he jangles back at motors in general, *Who knows*
What evil lurks in the hearts of men? but then, inscrutably,
Refusing to laugh like The Shadow. When he walks on the table
In a fantailed pigeon-toed shuffling strut, getting a taste
Of formica with his leathery tongue, he challenges me
Each morning to fight for my wife if I dare to come near her,
Ruffling his neck and hunching, beak open, his amber eyes
Contracting to malevolent points. I taught him everything
He knows, practically, *Fair and foul are near of kin!*
Including how to love her as he croons in her soft voice,
I'm a green bird, and how to test me for the dialectic hell of it,
What then? sang Plato's ghost, What then? as if I knew
The answer which Yeats in his finite wisdom forgot to teach me.

David Wagoner

The Extraordinary Production of Eggs From the Mouth

(Pearls of wisdom)

As he stands alone on stage, the Professor
Shows us he has nothing
Up his sleeve or under his coattails,
Then lowers his brows as seriously as a man
Thinking of being something else, and there,
Would you believe it, from between his lips
The white tip of an egg comes <u>mooning</u> out.

As softly as a hen, he seems to lay it
In his nested fingers. Another. He eggs us on
To laugh and gag for him, to cluck and crow
For the last things we expected or hoped for—

Conjuror
producing eggs
— posturing
Academic.

metaphor.

uses imagery.
gag double
meaning.

143

Eggs in both hands, in tophats and fishbowls—
Till he has so many he could quit forever.

But now with a flick of the wrist, seeming to think
Better of his wobbly bonewhite offspring,
He puts one into his mouth, and another,
And each one vanishes back where it came from
Till all his hatchwork has been laid to rest.
He comes to the footlights, gaping for applause,
And except for the pink, withdrawn, quivering tongue,
We see his mouth is absolutely empty.

David Wagoner

[handwritten annotation: sums up poem writers contempt for posturing academics —]

Three Boys

Through steel-hawser winds of winter
Sometimes we went—but it's the slack days
Of August I remember best. We'd saunter
Hot as cork through the fishermen, to laze
In the golden ropes at the jetty head
While the sea made its soft, immeasurable lead

And the only cloud was high-gliding gulls.
I would bask, and Jim sleep, and Michael see
Invisible shoals nudging the piles
For sandhoppers. His fog-horn voice would carry
Through the heat, to tell us of the wrasse,
Dragonfly gurnet, and vast uncatchable bass

He'd seen. I'd look. Perhaps there'd be a rind
Of lemon floating like a dead anemone
Under us : but nothing else. I didn't mind
When he said I'd looked too late—not many
Months before, I'd have sworn it was true
That I'd seen those miracle fishes too.

But Big Jim minded. He stretched, long as a man,
And yawned, and told me to tell the kid to go.
When I did, he tried not to cry, and ran
Crookedly to the last of a broken row
Of lobster-pots, and out of sight. Sundown
Came, the anglers packed their tackle, and alone

Then we'd wait for the ships to use the tide.
Each vessel was a triangle of lights,
Red for the port, green for the starboard side
And white at mast-head. Some foggy nights
They vanished, leaving Jim and me no choice
But to see them plain as the fish in Michael's voice.

Ted Walker

Rook Shoot

Against the evening light, strung
across banks of cumulus,
goitres of mistletoe hung
from the necks of poplars.
Higher, in elms, rookeries
knotted the topmost traceries,
rank and black like a cancered lung.

Always a restlessness turned
in the top of those tall trees:
even at rest the birds leaned,
lurching backwards as a breeze
blew fitful into their faces
scabrous with the rub of branches
jabbed. There was no comfort

up in those crowded tenements,
save the warmth sometimes of sun
cupped in Aprilled-out softness
of new leaves, barely green,

that soothed for a while the roughness
away. At a time of this
tenderness, the men came.

Quickly they did what they had
come to do. They had no need to kill,
but some part of them remembered
the need of a man to kill
and had brought them with their want
under the purple birds. They shot.
And one by one the dark parcels fell,

thudding, to cumber the ground
underfoot, twitching out the last
frenetic beat of wing and heart.
We, when the men had passed
on, stood a while to watch
some turning birds in the distance
gyrate nearer, nearer, land

indomitable under
the ravage, walk among
the spilt eggs, peck them, gather
sustenance enough to sing
a cracked, ragged song up in
the roomier trees, to begin
tomorrow a new growth all over.

Ted Walker

Easter Poem

I had gone on Easter Day
early and alone to be
beyond insidious bells
(that any other Sunday

I'd not hear) up to the hills
where are winds to blow away
commination. In the frail
first light I saw him, unreal
and sudden through lifting mist,
a fox on a barn door, nailed
like a coloured plaster Christ
in a Spanish shrine, his tail

coiled around his loins. Sideways
his head hung limply, his ears
snagged with burdock, his dry nose
plugged with black blood. For two days
he'd held the orthodox pose.
The endemic English noise

of Easter Sunday morning
was mixed in the mist swirling
and might have moved his stiff head.
Under the hill the ringing
had begun: and the sun rose red
on the stains of his bleeding.

I walked the length of the day's
obsession. At dusk I was
swallowed by the misted barn,
sucked by the peristalsis
of my fear that he had gone,
leaving nails for souvenirs.

But he was there still. I saw
no sign. He hung as before.
Only the wind had risen
to comb the thorns from his fur.
I left my superstition
stretched on the banging barn door.

Ted Walker

The émigrés

Visiting from Britain, I take my ease
In a Massachusetts yard. Willows
Have opened overnight along the ridge;
This is the second spring I've seen this year.
I watch as my once-English hostess
Moves across the shadow of the spruces
At her door. She calls her home a cottage
And puts on homeliness like a sweater.

She's tried, over and over, to grow grass
Around the place; grass, and a few roses,
And even, look, a bit of privet hedge
To remind her of home in Warwickshire.

She brings me bourbon in an ice-packed glass
And tinkles on about the neighbours' houses.
Americanisms glint like a badge
Pinned onto her. She much prefers life here,

She protests, remembering what life was
For her in England—the dirt, rising prices,
Always having to live at the edge
Of her nerves. Not to mention the weather.

I stir my drink. 'I'd not mind it either,
For a while,' I say. Martins lodge,
Like my swallows at home, in crevices
Of her roof. 'Oh, purple martins, those

Damn things. I'll have to rake them down from there,'
She says. 'Mind you, it's not that I begrudge
Them somewhere to live. But if you saw the mess
They make, you wouldn't think me heartless.'

Now, in his office near a fall-out shelter
High over downtown Boston, husband Reg
Will be turning his calendar (English Views
In Summertime) into May. The two of us,

Last evening, swept the last of the winter
Cones into a heap. Outside his garage
Afterwards, he told me, watching the flames,
Of all his new, perpetual worries:

There's his job—they daren't have kids. And Russia.
And how he'll never keep up with the mortgage.
Not to mention the droughts, the six-foot snows,
In the yard where nothing English ever grows.

Ted Walker

Self-Portrait at Ten

The whipped horse was lame. We'd cycled to town,
My aunt and myself. There, at a crossing
Lurched a ragpicker's cart and the lame horse
Dancing, as if crazed hornets flew
At its skin from all sides. The ragman's whip
Was old and broken, like the man
Himself, and the lame horse . . . And a crowd
Of tourists with melting cones silently
Melting away, quietly back to their cars.
We stopped by the horse. 'Stop that!' my aunt
Shouted; and the short whip
Fell across our shadows, stroke by stroke
Scored over the dust the horse's nerves at our feet.
And I think it didn't matter then,
But now it matters: what shock kept horses tame
Yet with every nerve gone wild under the whip,
Its eyes bone double worlds of scalding white
In the sun and dust. And the nag's
Tameness reached me; and my aunt's voice
Crying 'Stop that!' while my thumbs
Burned white on the cycle-grips, the whole sky
Waiting to burst and rain on the horse the cry in me.

David Wevill

Desperados

These four lie on a blanket,
A cluster of cactuses hides them from quick
Discovery and the road. Three are grown men,
Fat and moustached, stretched flat on their backs with eyes
Wide and staring, as if the sun
And not bullets had struck them dead.
The fourth, a child, lies closest in the photograph,
Her eyes half-shut with the instantaneous
Headache of lead. Now in this child's face
The crime folds its hands and waits—
Horror-struck. While somewhere in those far hills,
Baked white as the whitest bread,
Black figures with smoking pistols break
A cigarette and share it. Why did she die?
They do not ask now. They squat,
Hands slumped between their knees, waiting the outcry.
And it almost seems the photographer
Was the first one here: his silver shutter and lens
Piercing through flies and the blood
Caked on the child's face, gouted on the men's chests.
She was the child of this fat
Official she fell beside; whose round, greedy stare
Somehow smuggled his life out through his wounds
Past the customs of death. He looks surprised—
As if caught in a last act of graft—
And the child beside him, like a sick child,
His graft once protected. Together now
Their tragedy speaks more shrilly than in life:
Her trust, and his shrewd lack of it
Which bought bullets for both on a dusty road;
And the daughter entered her father's life
Without wincing . . . The other two don't count.
Their deaths enter the hills where the gunmen crouch.

David Wevill

Market Square

In the store window
behind yellow glass
two .38's, two .45's
          (one with a hand-stitched holster)
a blackjack, a row of flick-knives

all cheap at the price

ammunition boxed among
the dead wasps and flies
gunmetal, nickel plate
wood rubbed smooth and eaten into by sweat

such as shines
on the passing, reflected faces
who pause here . . .
                    And pause
at the store's other half

where behind the yellowing glass
the brothers Kennedy and Martin Luther King
stare beyond their portraits
blindly into the sun

their eyes not meeting the eyes

and an Easter message scrawled
in the same hand
that fixed the price on the guns—

'Brothers, remember and pray'

David Wevill

The Birth of a Shark

What had become of the young shark?
It was time for the ocean to move on.
Somehow, sheathed in the warm current
He'd lost his youthful bite, and fell
Shuddering among the feelers of kelp
And dragging weeds. His belly touched sand,
The shark ran aground on his shadow.

Shark-shape, he lay there.
But in the world above
Six white legs dangled, thrashing for the fun of it,
Fifty feet above the newborn shadow.

The shark nosed up to spy them out;
He rose slowly, a long grey feather
Slendering up through the dense air of the sea.
His eyes of bolted glass were fixed
On a roundness of sun and whetted flesh,
Glittering like stars above his small brain—

The shark rose gradually. He was half-grown,
About four feet: strength of a man's thigh
Wrapped in emery, his mouth a watery
Ash of brambles. As he rose
His shadow paled and entered the sand,
Dissolved, in the twinkling shoals of driftsand
Which his thrusting tail spawned.

This was the shark's birth in our world.

His grey parents had left him
Mysteriously and rapidly—
How else is a shark born?
They had bequeathed him the odour of blood,
And a sense half of anguish at being
Perpetually the forerunner of blood:

A desire to sleep in the currents fought
Against the strong enchaining links of hunger,
In shoals, or alone,
Cruising the white haze off Africa,
Bucked Gibraltar, rode into the Atlantic—
Diet of squid, pulps, a few sea-perch.

But what fish-sense the shark had
Died with his shadow. This commonplace
Of kicking legs he had never seen:
He was attracted. High above him
The sunsoaked heads were unaware of the shark—
He was something rising under their minds
You could not have told them about: grey thought
Beneath the fortnight's seaside spell—
A jagged effort to get at something painful.

He knew the path up was direct:
But the young shark was curious.
He dawdled awhile, circling like a bee
Above stems, cutting this new smell
From the water in shapes of fresh razors.
He wasn't even aware he would strike;
That triggered last thrust was beyond his edgy
Power to choose or predict. This
Was carefully to be savoured first, as later
He'd get it, with expertise, and hit fast.

He knew he was alone.
He knew he could only snap off
A foot or a hand at a time—
And without fuss—for sharks and dogs
Do not like to share.
The taste for killing was not even pleasure to him.
And this was new:
This was not sea-flesh, but a kind
Of smoky scent of suntan oil and salt,

Hot blood and wet cloth. When he struck at it
He only grazed his snout,
And skulked away like a pickpocket—

Swerved, paused, turned on his side,
And cocked a round eye up at the dense
Thrashings of frightened spray his climb touched.

And the thrashing commotion moved
Fast as fire away, on the surface of sun.
The shark lay puzzling
In the calm water ten feet down,
As the top of his eye exploded above
Reef and sand, heading for the shallows.
Here was his time of choice—
Twisting, he thought himself round and round
In a slow circling of doubt,
Powerless to be shark, a spawned insult.

But while he was thinking, the sea ahead of him
Suddenly reddened; and black
Shapes with snouts of blunted knives
Swarmed past him and struck
At the bladder of sunlight, snapping at it.
The shark was blinded—
His vision came to him,
Shred by piece, bone by bone
And fragments of bone. Instinctively
His jaws widened to take these crumbs
Of blood from the bigger, experienced jaws,
Whose aim lay in their twice-his-length
Trust in the body and shadow as one
Mouthful of mastery, speed, and blood—

He learned this, when they came for him;
The young shark found his shadow again.
He learned his place among the weeds.

David Wevill

Notes on the poets and poems

These notes will tell you basically four things: 1) a little about the poet himself; 2) what his poetry is about; 3) how he has made it, both from ideas and techniques and; 4) which other poets he is attached to. This last point will enable you to find and read more of the kind of poetry you like.

After the notes, there is a glossary, a list of words with which you may not be familiar, and which will explain further the notes and the art of the poet. Finally, for those of you who want to read a wider selection of poetry than is presented in this book, there is a bibliography of books by the poets. These books can either be bought through bookshops or ordered from a public library.

A word of warning, though: not all poetry is easy. It needs several readings to be appreciated so don't dismiss a poem (or a poet) because, at first sight, he or she seems to be not for you. Try several times (not one after the other) to reach through to the poem. If finally, you can't get anything out of it then pass on.

MARTIN BELL   *1918–1978*

Martin Bell served in the Royal Engineers during the Second World War, took a degree in English at Southampton, where he was born, and spent some years teaching in schools and at Leeds College of Art. He is an enigmatic figure and has published only two books of verse, yet he is an important poet for all that.

He lived in the 1930s, when many young men felt idealistically Socialist (he was a member of the Communist Party in that decade) and he looked up to those who fought Fascism in the Spanish Civil War. The second poem, *David Guest*, is about just such a person; it's an elegy that doesn't sing the praises of the man, but states how wrong he was to get killed, wasting his life. The poem attacks the pointlessness of his death and Bell is best when he writes attackingly, especially when he hits at false values or institutions as he does in *Headmaster: Modern Style*, his most famous poem. It was about a real character and the rumour goes that the poem actually killed him: he saw the poem lying on the staffroom table, went into a rage and suffered a stroke. How much truth there is in this is dubious. The point is though that the poem is vitriolic and harsh enough to make it possible. The imagery is cruel and the metaphors bitter. The diction is chosen so that the words sound sarcastic and the poem is best read out loud to gain the full benefit of the emotions. The blank verse form and the length of the poem make it doubly strong, as if the tedious

'Snitch' is doing part of the talking.

If ever there was a hate poem—as opposed to a love poem—then this is it. It holds all the power of Bell's poetry, the ability to strike home with an idea and make us see just what thoughts lie beneath the lines. Bell's dislike for this headmaster is certainly apparent.

JOHN BERRYMAN *1914–1972*

John Berryman committed suicide in January, 1972, by throwing himself off a bridge; his death greatly shocked the literary world for he is considered to be a major American poet and in a special mould. He is said to be one of the 'confessional' poets.

This term means that the poet uses his poetry in order to comment upon himself as a human, stepping outside his own skin, as it were, and looking back as if at another person. To do this well one needs to be a fine poet and Berryman is; he used a set formula for this, writing about a character called Henry who was himself. Occasionally, Henry became Mr. Bones as well. This *persona* (see Glossary) appeared widely in Berryman's life's work, his dream songs, a very long sequence of short poems of which two are included in this book. In all over 400 were published in addition to other Henry pieces. Becoming detached from himself, Berryman was able to be objective, look at his own weaknesses and strengths and, by writing about them, was able to accept them and himself for what he was. Many of the poems are humorous, as if Berryman was laughing aside at himself and they are written in a conversational style, as if the poet was actually talking.

However, a close look at the poems shows that under the apparently easy style of writing there is a very fine artistry. Strict rhyme-schemes appear, consonance and alliteration abound and the choice of words is expert, saying what is meant with a sharp clarity. Visual imagery is common, too and this is best shown here in the last poem.

Berryman was one day younger than—and a close friend of—the Welsh poet, Dylan Thomas. *In Memoriam (1914–1953)* is a beautifully sad poem about Thomas' death and their friendship. It is a very personal poem (notice how Berryman has left a space in the 8th. stanza rather than write Thomas' wife's name) yet it has a universal reach. The diction is unique in this poem, with Berryman inventing words to suit the emotion—'highlone' in line 3, and using italics as a means of stressing words as an instruction to the reading voice. The poem is most successful because of the pathos in it that is highlighted by the diction—'useless versus coma' and 'mid potpals' yapping'—and the terrible line: 'His bare stub feet stuck out.'

ROBERT BLY *1926–*

Living most of his life in Minnesota, in the virtual centre of the USA, Bly has become known as the leading poet in the move towards simplicity in poetry. He is not concerned in his work with deep messages and emotions, but with the portraying of life as it is, on its own terms. In this respect, he has similarities with Donald Hall and, to a lesser extent, William Stafford and a comparison of these three brings out just how well each writes in similar yet different manners.

Robert Bly went to several universities as a student (including Harvard) and served in the US Navy in the latter half of the Second World War. He lives now as a writer and translator, and as the latter he is very prolific and famous. He is also famous for having started the 'American Writers Against the Vietnam War' movement and the first poem is his best to come from this. It is a simple poem based upon the daily death-count given on American television at the height of that war, a macabre poem that has an undertone of sarcasm which places it as a major anti-war comment. What makes the poem work so well is the image of the dead becoming mere decoration and despite the use of exclamation marks, which suggest a kind-of celebration to the lines, an uplifting quality, there is a deep sense of melancholy present.

In *Sleet Storm on the Merritt Parkway*—the Parkway is a motorway for passenger cars only—Bly describes a drive in winter, how the houses look snug in the American Dream of freedom and comfort, but how they all become involved in wrangles of finances and madness; his poem is about the human condition, the harshness of reality in the harsh winter.

From concern with society, it is only a short step to being worried about pollution and, in *The Dead Seal . . .*, Bly describes a meeting with a seal being killed by oil pollution. He handles the event as a narrative poem in a prose-poem form and this makes it all the easier to grasp, especially when the seal's cries are given ('Awaark!') and the animal is compared to something we know—a car tyre inner-tube in section 2 or an ugly old lady. The relationship that the poet tries to build with the seal tells us what he felt, too—the guilt at having killed the creature, the need to return to see how the seal is the next day— and the seal's rejection is the final comment upon mankind, added to by the reference to the seal as a brother whom we have assassinated.

Bly's last poem here is a celebration of family life and it links in with *Driving towards the Lac Qui Parle River*, for both poems speak of the peace in natural things, be they a view or love. There is humour in *Coming In for Supper* and both poems have an air of calm about them.

Throughout the poems, Bly relies upon visual imagery—the giving of a picture so that the reader can literally see what is happening and, therefore, draw ideas or get nearer to the emotions involved. Bly's reading voice—strident but full of tone and emphasis—gives the poems an extra power, when read out loud.

RICHARD BRAUTIGAN *1933–*

Richard Brautigan still seems to be the young man of American poetry and his work is very young at heart in many ways. He first made his reputation as a novelist, writing in a unique (at the time almost experimental) manner with sparse diction and an aim to hit his readers with powerful, if somewhat obvious, imagery and 'message'.

The poetry is often humorous, with obvious emotional content and an easily understood meaning. In *The Chinese Checker Players*, the poetry is simple until the last line, where 'and cheated' carries so many meanings—did they enjoy cheating? did they cheat because life was cheating them? did they cheat for the excitement? This kind of questioning can go on and on—if you look at Stevie Smith's verse, you'll see that she writes like this. Brautigan is a poet who has come to the fore partly through the post-Beat poet era (see the notes on Allen Ginsberg) where poetry is trying to be less intellectual or 'brainy' and more importantly direct towards life as everyone lives it. His poetry makes a social comment, too—*On the Elevator Going Down* is a funny poem, but it has a serious ending. The first poem also appears humorous, a bit eccentric, but it has a beauty in its language and a subject with a sad ending that pushes other thoughts into our minds.

ALAN BROWNJOHN *1931–*

Alan Brownjohn is a social poet and can be compared to others like Philip Larkin. He mirrors and shows society through examples that are facets of the whole scene. He has been a teacher, a college lecturer, a city councillor, a poetry critic and editor, a Labour Party parliamentary candidate and is now a full-time writer.

Brownjohn's verse is typified by a quietness: unlike some other poets who also write on 'social themes', he does not shout out his message (see Adrian Mitchell for that!) or try to make it overdone and too simple. He would like us to think about his work, to ponder it and its implications. *1939* is just such a poem: a child (the poet was eight years old at the time) finds a badge, something boys treasured, and wants it badly for himself, but he doesn't take it. The morality in the poem is there and it contrasts with the year when war broke out and morality changed. It's a very moving poem, if thought about.

So is *Office Party*, with its strict rhyme scheme, its tongue-in-cheek humour and the pathos at the end; the poem depends upon visual imagery that is detailed but doesn't give the whole picture. It lays down guidelines that we can alter to suit our ideas as does *A202*, a poem based upon the road of that number through South London; the point here is to be found in the last verse—just let it be added that this road leads through the area where Alan Brownjohn was born.

CHARLES CAUSLEY *1917–*

Charles Causley is usually thought of as a children's poet, but in fact he was an adult writer long before that. He was in the Navy for most of the war and his most famous poem, *Song of the Dying Gunner AA1*, came from his naval experiences. Since 1947, he has been a junior school teacher (now headmaster) in his native Cornwall.

Causley is among the finest technical poets in Britain today: he has mastered verse technique and can handle rhyme, metre and every other skill with an unequalled dexterity. He has a Cornishman's feel for language and many of his poems, like *John Polruddon*, are rooted in legend, local stories or rural, West Country life in the early years of the century. His simple poems have a message and, in this respect, bear a similarity with fables—simplistic stories that educate. *The Animals' Carol* is perhaps the highlight of Causley's expertise. He writes a celebratory poem, with a rhyme scheme and perfect metrical structure, incorporating the Latin which adds depth and perception to the poem which was, when it was first published, printed with full colour plates. The alliterative quality of the Latin phrases (the words on the right are a translation of the Latin) gives the poem a lyrical quality and, in many cases, the Latin is also semi-onomatopœic, for 'Christus natus est!' sounds a little like a cockerel's crowing.

DOUGLAS DUNN *1942–*

In his first book, *Terry Street*, Douglas Dunn wrote a sequence of poems about working class life in a city area and they earned him an immediate reputation as a social poet, compared by many to Philip Larkin, for his work sought to look not so much at situations (as Alan Brownjohn's verse does) but at people.

The Wealth is an unusual poem, for Dunn has succeeded here in writing one of the few poems about the rock music world, basing his ideas upon the life of Paul Simon, of Simon and Garfunkel fame. The poem is stark and full of despair, with harsh language and actions and it uses allusion to a great extent for its impact, both literary and of place and event. In order to be fully understood, the poem has to be read several times and is not easy then—the references to medical examinations, American writers (Lowell, Cooper), the military call-up, the emigrating Jews and the anachronisms are confusing at first, but become clearer.

Dunn doesn't seek to cover up what he observes: he writes of scenes in a realistic manner that in no way flatters. In the second poem, *Young Women in Rollers*, he even draws to our attention that they are 'The type who burst each other's blackheads/In the street and look in handbag mirrors.' The poet sees these people as living in a world apart from others, including himself.

ALLEN GINSBERG *1926–*

In 1970, Allen Ginsberg described himself as a Beat-Hip-Gnostic-Imagist. He was the leading light of the Beat Movement of poetry in the Fifties and Sixties and is still a major influence today. He was born in New Jersey and when he was thirty, he published *Howl and Other Poems*, an outspoken book that took America by storm, creating controversy and literary scandal for Ginsberg's style was refreshing, avant garde and brash. With other writers like Jack Kerouac, Lawrence Ferlinghetti and William Burroughs, Ginsberg started a new direction in poetry writing, a style that was rich with imagery, esoteric knowledge and often outrageous subject matter which both shocked and enlightened the public.

Drawing upon Buddhist philosophy, jazz music, American urban life and shamanism (a primitive, Siberian religion where the spirits are controlled by shamen, or medicine men), Ginsberg's verse is ebullient, energetic and exciting. He has travelled widely, as a writer giving performances (for which he is internationally famous) or as a literary tourist, expanding his knowledge. This shows in his poems that range from being about Ankor Wat (the ruined city in South-East Asia) to London, Cambridge, Australia, New York. In each poem, as in *Mugging*, there come together influences from all over the world to give the work a universality of purpose and idea. *Mugging* is about the poet being 'mugged' in New York and holds his fears, the horror of the situation, and the attitudes towards it that he and passers-by felt: he tries to calm himself with a mantra (a prayer)—'Om Ah Hum'—and, finally, he draws the ironic conclusion that the thieves missed his valuable poems in his shoulder bag.

Father Death Blues is a poem, like many of Ginsberg's, that is intended to be seen as a chant or song and even has musical notation with it. Ginsberg uses rhyme in the poem just as a jazz song-writer would. In the final poem, *Written on Hotel Napkin: Chicago Futures*, the poet is criticizing and outlining American life with humour and pathos.

DONALD HALL   *1928–*

For many years a university professor in the USA, Donald Hall is now a full-time writer on his grandfather's farm in New Hampshire. Hall is a truly trans-Atlantic poet, for he was educated at American universities and Oxford (where he won the Newdigate Prize for poetry), has lived in England and was first published as a poet in Britain.

Of the four poems included in this book, two are of British origin and two American: the British ones both deal with the poet looking at old wartime air-fields and are interesting for they show how widely poetic ideas can come from similar subject matter. *An Airstrip in Essex, 1960* is a nostalgic poem which is largely reportage save for the emotive last stanza, whilst *The Old Pilot's Death* is much more far-reaching in its aims. An old man returns to an air-field and, in a dream that becomes his death, he flies again with exhilaration to join a host of others rising into heaven: the last four lines are movingly written and mysteriously made to give a sense of visual import, like angels riding on sunbeams in Victorian, religious paintings.
The two American poems are about Hall's family home. Both look at family history and how the poet relates himself to his ancestors through the link they have with the land. Again, there is nostalgia at work, but it is firmly used and the work avoids sentimentality. *The Farm* has one central subject to each verse—the wind, the old man, The Pennacook, the lake and fish—and they are all joined by time passing but impinging upon Hall himself. *Maple Syrup* is one of the poet's best works. The syrup is sweet and delicious, made from the sap of maple trees by many New England farmers and it is used as an image of the sweetness of human life and love. Hall and his wife are unable to trace the grandfather's grave and this saddens them but, in the house, they find some of his syrup and in it they can share something real and binding with the dead man. Hall communicates with his grandfather in a tangible manner, the sweet syrup killing the bitterness of death. The poem's success lies in its description and plain way of dealing with narrative which holds more than a tale, for the emotion is one we can easily identify with at a personal level.

SEAMUS HEANEY *1939–*

Seamus Heaney was born in County Derry, educated in Derry and Queen's University, Belfast and has spent much of the time since as a university lecturer.

Heaney captures with succinct observation the atmosphere of Irish life and the kind of history Ireland holds, be that ancient and concerning the Celtic twilight or modern and the troubles in Ulster. *The Grauballe Man* fits the first category, although it is actually about a peat-bog burial in Denmark: some years ago, excavations revealed a large number of pre-Roman and Dark Ages burials, many of them sacrificial, and most of them in an excellent state of preservation due to trace elements in the boggy soil. Heaney first came across these burials in a book called 'The Bog People' (by P. V. Glob) and was immediately struck by the coming face to face with Iron Age men and women of whom the first documented find was in County Down.

A New Song, with its abab rhyme scheme (some of the rhymes are half-rhymes) celebrates rural Ireland as do *Follower* and *The Outlaw*, each having a more direct, autobiographical basis and metrical structures to suit the subject matter. *Follower* has a sad ending to it and shows well the relationship between a father and son: *The Outlaw* is faintly humorous, but mostly gentle and improved by the appropriate diction—'flank/tank' for the hard activity of the mating bull, 'wall/stall' to strengthen the action of the door and thunderous bull and 'outlaw/straw' for the final retreat into the dark barn. Notice that the cadence of the rhyming words carries a big responsibility for the effect of the rhyme and the sense of the poem.

The final poem, from a sequence entitled, *Singing School*, writes obliquely about the Ulster troubles and captures the emotiveness of an Orange parade.

Moyola = an area of Co. Derry; bawn and rath = fortified and ancient enclosures; lambeg = a kind of drum.

WILLIAM HEYEN *1940–*

William Heyen grew up on Long Island and his work has its roots in history, the countryside and the family. He writes in traditional forms, using rhyme expertly (though often not in strict schematics—see *Driving at Dawn*) and keeping to metrical shapes. He uses imagery in an exacting manner (*Spring*) and utilises legends for a medium of expression (*Legend of the Tree at the Center of the World*). He experiments with form: *Mantle*, about a famous baseball player of that name, is curved like the flight of a pitched baseball. He uses dreams to explain everyday realities (*Son Dream*) and feelings (*Pet's Death*) to himself and his readers and he seeks to recapture lost happiness founded in peace and childhood (*Worming at Short Beach*).

Heyen's poetry has no pretensions and it doesn't try to force itself upon the audience. In this respect it is similar to William Stafford's work and it is a good exercise to compare some of Heyen's poems with Robert Bly's and Stafford's, especially *Traveling Through the Dark*.

TED HUGHES 1930–

Ted Hughes was born in Yorkshire and educated at a local grammar school and Pembroke College, Cambridge. For a while, he taught, was in the RAF, worked as a rose gardener and a night-watchman and turned professional writer. He also farms in Devonshire. Hughes is, without doubt, the most important British poet alive today and will probably prove in time to be one of the most important of this century.

His poetry is characterized by its powerful language, its fascination with nature, mythology and humanity seen through a vision of brutal activity, violence and force. His work is strongly visual and often described as elemental, for it deals in the foundation markers of existence. In his collection, *Crow*, Hughes is fascinated by primitive concepts of life and death. His poetry is aided in its directness by being a part of the oral tradition of modern poetry, demanding to be heard as well as read on the page—Hughes is one of the best poetry readers in the world. Since *Crow*, published in 1970, Hughes has gone in two different directions with his verse. One is towards a deeper involvement with primitive ideas and forces, the other moves away from this towards a study of nature, the past and human relationships.

A Bedtime Story comes from *Crow*. It is vividly imagistic and macabre with many layers of meaning to it; it is incantatory and has the feel of a spell about it, the repetition allowing it to be read with a chant-like insistence. *Wodwo* has similar qualities and is written in the first person by an unknown, bestial animal, seeking for some primeval truth—a 'wodwo' is assumed to be a kind of wild man: it is an Anglo-Saxon word for which no accurate translation has been found. The lack of a good deal of punctuation forces the poem to read continuously, with breaks coming at the line ends in places, so that the whole has a metre similar to the actions of an animal routing in the woods.

The macabre affects even Hughes' poetry for children. *The Burrow Wolf* is a comic-strip beast that lives on the moon. The poem uses alliteration and sibilance for effect and yet, although it is humorous, it is also like *Wodwo* threatening and hinting at fear.

Although Hughes' mystical poetry can be hard to understand, this is not so in his writing about natural forces and experience, even when the poems still contain mystical elements. Written in blank verse, *A Solstice* is just such a poem, a narrative piece about walking in mid-winter and shooting a fox. The description is rich, enhanced by colour imagery and personae—the fox as an elegant gentleman, the gun as a predatory hunter. The ending is powerful and the metaphors (his 'bag of useless jewels') so strong as to wrench. There is a morality at work, too—Hughes' brother, after living abroad for 18 years, has behaved like too many humans and killed his ancestry ('your first real Ancient Briton') in a reflex action. The last line condemns in its detachment, yet indicates how the killing numbed the two men.

Symbolism is used by Hughes. *A motorbike*, a true story, uses the machine as a symbol for power, freedom and death, the excitement men seek and feel a lack of in peace-time. *Tractor*, with its accurate diction and onomatopæia ('The starting lever cracks its action, like a snapping knuckle'), stands for the fight between machinery and nature, but can be taken as a simple description of starting a tractor on a winter morning: one might say the best poetry is that which has two (or more) levels of meaning.

The final poem develops from rural life, as does *Tractor*. *Cock-Crows* has Hughes standing on a Yorkshire moorland rim, looking down into the industrial valley, hearing the bird calls and seeing these as indicative of nature overcoming the grime of industrial life, yet comparing it with it—the cockcrows like 'Lobbed-up horse-shoes of glow-swollen metal'. The poet is writing about Hebden Bridge. One can see, in this astonishing use of language, just how Hughes has gained his massive reputation. He has the ability to take himself into a different plane of reality, and us with him, the act of the true poet.

GALWAY KINNELL   *1927–*

Galway Kinnell was born in Providence, Rhode Island. His work links up with that of Robert Bly, William Stafford and William Heyen to form the modern, American tradition.

This tradition involves a number of major factors: criticism of American life and appreciation of the more important sense of values, an interest in nature and 'the wild' and its relationship to men, a seeking for personal and national identity, and a celebration of beauty, both man-made and otherwise. Kinnell's verse shows all of these characteristics.

The River that is East is about the East River in New York, which separates Manhattan and Bronx from Queens and Brooklyn on Long Island. Kinnell approaches his subject matter in two ways: he lists images so that emotional response is made and he draws upon comparison and allusion to heighten this. Even if one is unaware of the actual implications of the images prompted by such as Gatsby, Grant and the Jamaica Local, the sense that these bring aids in understanding. Hence an esoteric and very 'American' poem becomes universal.

The lists of images appear again in *Spindrift*—the word refers to heavily driven sea spray. Alliteration adds to the reportage effect ('Pluck sacred/Shells from the icy surf'). Halfway through, the image of the sea prompts new trains of thought and the poet passes onto considering old age, death and loss and, in this respect, the poem is a kind of stream of consciousness work which is both personal and impersonal. Landscape sets a mood from which the poetry springs—as in Bly's *Driving towards the Lac Qui Parle River*.

Tree from Andalusia is a similarly personal poem but with two new techniques also appearing—the introduction of natural music in the wind, giving it a tonal quality that builds on the emotion, and the use of a foreign language for its musical content, regardless of its meaning. Kinnell has used this trick a good deal and with considerable effect.

Kinnell's most famous poem is *The Bear*. The poet as hunter is an idea that is common in American verse and British work, too (look at Hughes' *A Solstice*, for example) and it brings together the animalistic side of mankind with his civilized side. Kinnell writes in a dream-like stance, outlining the trapping and tracking of the bear, the use of its body for protection against the vicious winter and the manner in which the man becomes the bear, by eating it and using its body as his own. At the end, he metamorphoses into the bear and draws the parallel that poetry is the stuff of existence. The poem is tough and harsh, the action brutal and the diction matches it. As in the other poems, the images are important and whereas lists of objects are used elsewhere, here it is a listing of activity that builds to the climax.

PHILIP LARKIN *1922–*

Although Philip Larkin has published only four main collections of verse, his poetic reputation is extensive. He has spent most of his working life as a university librarian, with two novels and a large volume of jazz writings behind him, in addition to his poetry.

Mr Bleaney has a melancholic air about it, in common with much of Larkin's verse which takes a sidelong look at society, studying its weaknesses and often seamier sides. Here the poet has taken over the dead Bleaney's one-room lodging and uses this as a medium to comment upon the human condition. A tight control of metrical form and rhyme scheme (abab) are also Larkin's strong points. *Going, going* was commissioned to be written by the Department of the Environment and appeared in a publication entitled, 'How do you want to live?' It plays on the words of the auctioneer—'Going, going—gone!' and is a wry and sorry comment upon general pollution. The poem is written in sestets (six line stanzas) with a regular abcabc rhyme, except for a slight change in the second stanza; it is a sign of a good poem that nothing seems forced when reading it, although the pattern is rigidly adhered to. In stanza 6, there is a caesura, a cut in mid-line which here makes the reader jump from the present awefulness to the future world. Pessimism and ironic attitudes are a common factor in Larkin's work.

The second poem, *The Explosion*, is untypical of Larkin. It has no rhyme scheme (though it is metrically solid) and it is not pessimistic, but full of hope, the lark's eggs symbolic of beauty and life in the wasteland of disaster and death that lurks beneath the fine, summer's day.

GEORGE MACBETH   *1932–*

George MacBeth is a very wide-reaching writer. From 1958–76, he was a major poetry producer for the BBC and it was largely due to him that poetry received so much broadcasting time in those years. At the same time he was building up a substantial reputation as a poet. Since 1954 he has published over 20 full-length verse collections, several novels and children's verse books, and edited a large number of anthologies. He has also written radio feature programmes, some plays and an opera.

For range, few can equal his poetry which runs from the moving through the humorous, to the macabre. He has written experimental sound poetry, on the very fringes of the avant garde and yet he has also written tightly structured verse using intricate rhyme schemes, metres and internal rhymes. There are few verse forms MacBeth cannot use with talented skill.

Death of a Ferrari is a humorous poem with pathos and laments the passing of the poet's car, a Ferrari which caused him infinite trouble and yet which he—like the owners of many such expensive racing saloons—loved. It is written in blank verse, in the modern sense of the term, and is basically a narrative poem. So is *Poem for Breathing* which is based upon an actual event. The end of this poem might seem puzzling on the page, but like all MacBeth's work it is intended not only for reading but for public performance. As a performer, MacBeth is one of the foremost British exponents of verse readings and he seeks audience participation as an adjunct to his work.

In *The Land-mine*, which is written in a similar form to Larkin's *Going, Going*, MacBeth is dealing with the bombing of his childhood home in semi-surrealist terms. The first three lines are nightmarish and set the scene for the poem which ends with the poet considering his own death. It is an example of the macabre, surreal side to MacBeth which also appears in *A True Story* (which is true!) and *Marshall*, with its alliteration, mockery and anti-climax, both written for performance.

ADRIAN MITCHELL   *1932*–

Like George MacBeth, Adrian Mitchell's verse is best in live performance and it also contains the elements of macabre thought and surreal imagery.

After leaving university, Mitchell spent many years as a newspaper journalist and his poetry carries the stamp of journalistic writing. Mitchell's poetry has the pull of newspaper headlines, the immediacy of comment and the obvious presentation of facts and 'message'. *Open Day at Porton*, not a likely event, as Porton Down is the top secret, biological warfare laboratory, is about a biological or chemical weapon and its ultimate effect . . . the moral of the poem, which is a kind of fable, is left to us to decide: fight madness with madness?

Not all Mitchell's verse is so harshly obvious; he can be subtle and then the pathos, understanding of humanity and emotion come through all the better. *Dumb Insolence* with its humour, is a sad poem which needs no explanation and has an obvious social message. As the social poet, Mitchell is well-known for poems like *Old Age Report* where the humour ('dust the cat') deliberately falls flat and the subject matter is both touchingly and forcefully stated with little embellishment. Finally, *Lady Macbeth in the Saloon Bar Afterwards*: one of Mitchell's funniest poems about a Shakespearean actress talking about a school matinée performance of *Macbeth*. Like all of Mitchell's poems, it has that ring of truth which is hilarious and slapstick here and very un-funny in *Old Age Report*.

BRIAN PATTEN   *1946–*

In the mid-Sixties, under the wave of The Beatles and 'Liverpool Culture', there developed 'The Liverpool Poets'—Roger McGough, Adrian Henri and Brian Patten. They came from the fringes of the pop world in a way, their poetry being an extension of the music of the times, if not in structure then certainly in subject-matter and popular approach. (McGough went into the music world as well as the literary one, with a group called 'Scaffold' which reached the hit parade on more than one occasion.')

Brian Patten has worked mainly as a writer since leaving school and his reputation was made on his first two books (which portrayed youth as he saw it and lived it) and his public readings. He has published five verse collections and a number of children's books. His poetry can be sentimental and weak, but even when it is, it carries a strain of youthful reality in it that tends to nullify the poor writing. *Old Crock* is about ageing and Patten uses the metaphor of an astronaut and his memories to highlight the depression and fear of death. *Little Johnny's Final Letter* is about reaching adulthood and it has a macabre, horrible quality to it, like a kidnap ransom note in a way. *A Blade of Grass* is sentimental and the idea is almost a cliché but it somehow seems to work, to be successful in the last few lines, a comment upon growing up. *Albatross Ramble* is humorous, even comic, on one level and the narrative style makes this plain: yet the albatross is a symbol for bad luck—one must never kill it for fear of eternal bad fortune—and here in the poem, it is the embodiment of that bad luck which lives with one and which one cannot be rid of: the message at the end is to accept it and wait for it to pass by.

SYLVIA PLATH   *1932–1963*

When Sylvia Plath died, only one of her books of poetry had been published; however, it brought her to the forefront of literary life. She was the daughter of a middle-class American couple, her father having been naturalized from German/Polish nationality, and proved to be a very clever child, passing from school to university where she obtained top grades: she subsequently attended Cambridge University where she met and married Ted Hughes. Together, they were to make a formidable and influential literary couple.

All of Sylvia Plath's poetry in this book coincides chronologically with the first years of Ted Hughes' writing and there are many similarities, for both wrote for each other, showing their work to their partners. After living in the USA for a short while and London, they bought an old, thatched house in Devon and Sylvia Plath's poetry began to absorb the natural world to a greater extent than previously. *The Arrival of the Bee Box* has an obvious subject to it, the purchase of a swarm of bees to establish in a hive, yet under the narrative there is a hidden threat, a suppressed violence that verges on fear. This is present in *The Rabbit Catcher* and, to some extent, in *Pheasant*. Sylvia Plath was able to relate herself closely with the world around her and she identifies with the bird in the poem as readily as she does with the dead in *All the Dead Dears*.

Death is a strong driving force in the poems and it was something that held Sylvia Plath's literary attention. Where many see death as an act of destruction, she saw it as a creative, artistic power and it featured as such in her work: in *The Goring* she sees the bull's attack on the picador (who enrages the bull with little spears to get it fighting mad with pain for the matador) not as a revenge, but as part of the dance towards a ritual death. *Old Ladies' Home* is a grim death-study of an old folk's home and the imagery is grotesque—'At owl-call the old ghosts flock' and 'And Death, that bald-headed buzzard'. The diction, as in all the poems, is superb.

No-one can pretend that Sylvia Plath's poetry is easy. It has a beautiful weirdness to it, an inviting malevolence that the world is dark, like a gorgeous flower that can kill you with its perfume, and it seeks to set a mood as much as tell of something concrete. It is highly personal, verging on the confessional, and yet it is equally impersonal and applicable to a wide range of people. It is sometimes hard to understand but the effort needed to come to terms with it is well worth the while.

PETER REDGROVE *1932–*

Formerly a scientific journalist, Peter Redgrove has lived as a writer now for many years. He is well-known as a surreal imagist, with a large number of poetry books to his credit as well as some strange yet fascinating novels, the first of which won the Guardian Fiction Award in 1973. He uses symbols in his poetry which delves into the world of the para-psychologist and the 'inner lives' which we all lead under our consciousness and his work seeks not only to entertain and teach in a broad sense, but also to enlighten us as to what goes on in the deeper corners of our mind.

Thirteen Ways of Looking at a Blackboard, from an early collection of Redgrove's poems, indicates just how this poet can see beneath the surface of ordinary objects and this also becomes apparent in *At the Edge of the Wood*, a comment upon time passing and the re-establishment of nature. Redgrove has been compared to Ted Hughes (to some extent) and *A Storm* justifies this, with heavy weather taking on the persona of a strangler while the tree becomes a woman—think how Hughes regards the fox. *Gentlemen* is a sardonic look at businessmen going to work, who are far from gentlemanly in their thoughts. *Design* is another poem with a hint (for it comes from an early book, like the first poem) of the surreal aspects to come in the poet's later work and which show through the magic in *Who's Your Daddy?*

PENELOPE SHUTTLE   *1947–*

Penelope Shuttle began writing when she was 14 and her first novel appeared when she was 17: others have come since. She has written poetry all along and is one of the foremost young women poets in Britain.

Her poetry is original and relies for effect upon visual and colour imagery, an eye for detail, an awareness of symbolism and a sense of wonderment, a sort of magical mysteriousness. Her work is not easy to understand and often operates in the mind like an abstract painting does—it aims not to give a picture so much as an atmosphere. What is of interest is that all of Penelope Shuttle's poems printed here have been written since she has been living and writing in close partnership with Peter Redgrove and show just how one author can influence another without that other losing their own identity. It is important to compare the two poets' work yet not lose sight of each as being in its own right.

ALAN SILLITOE   *1928–*

Best known as the novelist of *The Loneliness of the Long Distance Runner* and *Saturday Night and Sunday Morning*, Alan Sillitoe was born in Nottingham and left school at 14. He has spent most of his life as a writer, though, upon leaving school, he did spend some years working in a factory and as a radio operator in the RAF.

Sillitoe sees poetry as a means of expressing emotions which cannot be done justice to in other literary media. *Autumn*, which comes from the poet's childhood experiences in a working-class background, has a degree of impatience about it, of movement of the kind young people feel. This sense of activity is shared by *The River has Burst its Banks* and one can see how the emotions here would be hard put to be successful in prose which, being longer, would lose the impact of flood motion. In *Alchemist* the poet, as a child, melts down his toy soldiers but finally doesn't know what to remodel them as: he implies that they were at least frozen into war shapes when soldiers, but are now shapeless. The shapelessness gives them vast possibilities, like swords changed into peaceful ploughs. That a highly skilled novelist turns to poetry as a better means of saying what he thinks should be said only goes to prove the range and versatility of poetry over the other literary arts.

ROBIN SKELTON *1925–*

Although born in East Yorkshire, Robin Skelton is now considered to be a Canadian poet. He has taught in a Canadian university for over fifteen years and has taken Canadian citizenship. He has written many books of verse, and edited several poetry anthologies, and an internationally renowned literary magazine. He sees poetry as a universal art that can cut across national and cultural borders. Poetry to him is the ultimate in human, emotional expression.

It is almost an insult to use only three of his poems here, for he must have published well over 500. He is a poet who is amongst the best at writing narrative verse so that—in the truest sense of the idea of such poetry—it not only tells a story but becomes a commentary on human activity. It is best to let his poems speak for themselves and just give hints to help textual understanding.

The Friday Fish: madrona = an evergreen, hardwood tree from British Columbia, where the poet lives, writes and works; Reservation = Indian reservation; jig = a way of fishing; wire trace = a wire type of fishing line; dogfish = species of shark; mica = a flaky, shiny mineral.

John Arthur: Gnomon = an L-shaped object, like a carpenter's square; wreckers = beachcombers or people who make a living out of wrecks (wreckers' harvest = storm and the flotsam and jetsam from it); Lear = Shakespeare's King Lear, who at one stage of the play goes mad on a stormed-tossed heathland.

Ballad of Billy Barker: (look up the meaning of ballad in the glossary) ass = North American slang for bum; gulch = a narrow valley which often contained gold; The Fraser = a river; swaled = a coinage by the poet (possibly) to mean the rain came down solidly (swale means timber planking) or the rain swayed to and fro; decide yourself which might be the best interpretation; quartz = a milky-coloured stone which is translucent; Victoria = a city in British Columbia, Canada; pans = gold panning dishes; drouth = drought.

Ballad of Billy Barker is the finest, non-contemporary poem to be written about any of the North American gold rushes, and it is a major poem in the modern ballad form.

KEN SMITH   *1938–*

Ken Smith is another trans-Atlantic poet. He was born in Yorkshire and, after doing his national service and graduating from Leeds University, he became a teacher, an editor (of Britain's foremost literary magazine, 'Stand'), a barman and a BBC reader before going to live in America as a university lecturer and visiting writer. He now lives as a full-time writer.

His poetry is concerned with the environment (both natural and human), the historical past and the sense of living. His work is quietly passionate (look at *The Pity*, based upon a poem by Mao Tse-tung) and intense and often has at its core the struggle for survival of the individual person. The syntax of his poetry is formalized and yet has the looseness of the spoken word. His diction is exacting.

In *The Hunter*, one senses a debt to the poetry of Ted Hughes in the manner or style of writing. This is echoed in *Spring Poem*, which is a pastoral poem that shares stylistic traits with the work of Galway Kinnell: a comparison between these poets would not be a wasted exercise. Smith's concern with the link between history and the present shows up in *A description of the Lichway* ... which is about an actual track over Dartmoor. Placenames build up atmosphere and the dead come to life not as ghosts, but as the makers of the past, from which the present (and the present human condition) arose. The poem has an added effectiveness in that it discusses moorland life (the dead were stored in barrels of brine or, if wealthy, brandy, because the ground was too hard to be dug by the sexton) and relates this to the ever-present impression that the ancestors have made upon the earth.

STEVIE SMITH   *1902–1971*

People who knew or heard Stevie Smith reading her own verse cannot now look at her work in print without hearing again her very distinctive voice. Fortunately, she recorded a large body of her verse and it would be best to listen to a record on tape after the poems have been read here. (See p. 189)

Stevie Smith was a slight woman, thin and as active as a sparrow. She was widely loved in the literary world and, since her death, a stage-play (and film) based upon her life have been box office hits. She lived the life of the eccentric, staying for many years with an aged aunt.

At first glance, her poetry seems child-like if not childish, with rhymes that might have come from the poetry of Edward Lear or a nine-year-old. The subject matter appears just as child-like in some of the poems: *The Wild Dog* and *Croft* are examples of this. But the poems have a striking originality and freshness to them (like the innocent freshness of children's verse) and, underneath, they have sometimes macabre ideas, love and pathos. (Is Croft soft in the head? Soft and easily damaged by reality and so hiding?) *The Jungle Husband* is a letter from a husband away from his wife, in a ludicrous situation, but recalling her with affection. The humour counter-balances the sorrow which, in the end, is the dominant emotion, as it is in the poignant poem of loss, *Widowhood*.

Not Waving but Drowning is Stevie Smith's most famous poem. It does not try to do anything but make a comment on existence, with its abcb rhyme scheme, its uneven metre and—when heard read by the poet—the unusual stressing of certain syllables.

(The German in *Widowhood* roughly translates as: 'Oh! how dreadful, to be so old, with those dreadful bags under the eyes, as if she had cried a lot!' It is repeated, slightly altered, in verse 4.)

WILLIAM STAFFORD *1914–*

William Stafford was born in Kansas and after being university educated, became a conscientious objector in World War 2; he has been active in pacifist organizations since then. In this respect, there is a firm artistic and humanist tie between him and Robert Bly which is strengthened by the initial poem which bears resemblance to Bly's *The Dead Seal. Traveling Through the Dark* is a narrative poem about finding a dead but pregnant deer on a winter road and accepting the role of life- or death-giver to the still-to-be-born fawn; the title is ambiguous for the travelling is both through the dark night and the dark decision of deliberation to kill.

Whilst the first is a sad poem, or one that promotes sombre thoughts, the others are celebratory. *Montana Eclogue* is a good example with its atmosphere of guiding advice to those who have not experienced the wilds and the calm they hold. *Ice-Fishing* furthers this theme of quietude using rhyme and, like all other poems, the constructions of everyday speech for greater effect. *In the Old Days* and *They Say* contain humour that is wry and withdrawn (though none the less effective for that) in the former with a sound invocation of childhood and, in the latter, mingled with wonder at the magic that music can hold, that other 'country beyond all of those' where art and beauty and calmness reign.

All of Stafford's work has a sense of tranquillity, amity and concord running through it which has greatly influenced other writers like William Heyen and (to some extent) Robert Bly.

R. S. THOMAS *1913–*

In 1935, R. S. Thomas obtained a degree in Classics at University College, Bangor and, the following year, was ordained; he has lived since then as a parish priest in his native Wales and has become known as one of the major Welsh poets of this century, and an avid supporter of Welsh nationalism and heritage.

R. S. Thomas' poetry is set in Wales and contains the atmosphere of that country as much as Heaney's work does of Ireland. The background is usually rural and studies not only the place, but the inhabitants that people it and the emotions that govern their lives. Yet the poems also make a deliberate comment upon religion, the place of God in our lives (or, if not God, then holiness and its companion, beauty) and the need we have to realize this.

On the Farm is a typical Thomas poem: the subject matter is plain to see—the girl brings light into the lives of the three poor farm workers. She is a salvation of sorts, just as, in *Lore*, Job Davies is, with his natural optimism and rough code of rules to live by. (Lore is a natural law.) The sense of divinity is a feature of Thomas' poetry and *The Moor*, with its closeness to nature and God, gives this, the idea strengthened by the use of religious imagery—the breaking of bread, a kind of benediction. Finally, *Ravens*, which is a poem which owes much to the Welsh love of myth and which relates, without an obvious religious theme, the present-day view of ravens with a legendary tale. The colour imagery, though, suggests evil, heightened by such lines as 'the sly connoisseurs of carrion' and the birds as 'desultory flags of darkness'; the mention of innocence gives the poem a moral tone—the birds have somehow broken up the friendship.

DAVID WAGONER *1926–*

David Wagoner is an American poet whose work has similarities to Bly's, Kinnell's and Wevill's poetry. He lives as a university teacher and his poetry is influenced by his environment, for many years the state of Washington: it is a useful poetic exercise to see all these poets' work in comparison. Wagoner is also a magazine editor and a novelist.

His poetry has an air of mystery about it and this gives it a dramatic quality which is at once stimulating and intriguing. *Waiting with the Snowy Owls* has this dramatic tendency which is halted in the last line where the bathos becomes the poem's power, where Wagoner has his feelings destroyed by the misery of these extraordinarily fine birds penned up in a zoo. *Trying to Think by a Steel Mill*, a poem about thought and peacefulness, is even more dramatic, the form of the poem taking on the force of a stage speech. The diction is reliant upon the spoken voice for effect—reading the first verse aloud will demonstrate how much the tongue and throat have to work to make the words. The poems are not without humour, though this is ironic in *Talking Back* where the parrot, taught 'everything he knows' by the poet, does not know the ultimate truth which neither of them have—Yeats, the mystical and patriotic Irish poet, didn't teach it to Wagoner either. The poem is an oblique attack on education, whether intentional or not. *The Extraordinary Production of Eggs From The Mouth* is another poem like *Talking Back*: it describes a magician's act but—and this illustrates the power and possibility of poetry—one word gives the whole thing an ambiguity. It is 'professor'. Another attack at empty education? A mouth, pink and absolutely void? Of eggs, images of creation (note the homograph—eggs us on and birds' eggs), being just trickery? Eggs as giving birth to creatures and ideas?

TED WALKER   *1934–*

Ted Walker is a modern linguist, with several European languages in his grasp. He was born in Sussex where he has lived a good deal of his life, as a teacher and writer: he sees himself as a poet whose 'territory is Sussex and the Sussex coast'. Yet, like R. S. Thomas whose territory is also quite small, Walker's poetry has a universal range to it and it is this that makes him a fine writer.

He writes verse that has many common factors shared with Ted Hughes, others that are to be found in poems by Wevill, Plath, Bly, Ken Smith . . . which is really to show to what extent poetic minds cross-pollinate each other.

Three boys, about childhood turning to adulthood, about dreams and about (in the last stanza) the influence of one person on another, has techniques that are to be found in Hughes' *Tractor*: 'steel-hawser winds' and 'fog-horn voice'. *Rook Shoot* has an uneasiness about it, a feeling of violence and macabre horror—the nests like parts of a cancerous lung, the birds' faces scabrous (which means uneven or knobbly, but implies here covered with scabs), the birds as 'dark parcels' falling to 'cumber on the ground' where the diction is so evocative. (Cumber = to hinder, obstruct or make numb.) The ending is horrible and savage with the men killing the birds needlessly which, in turn, eat of their own eggs to keep their race going.

Easter Poem, which does not try to confuse the religious issue involved, is one of Walker's most famous poems. Once again, the diction is very good—'the peristalsis of my fear' (the meaning of peristalsis here is important)—and the poem's ending contains a lesson, an undertone of catharsis, in that the poem has cleared the writer's mind of something that he was thinking about and at loggerheads with. *The émigrés* is about an English couple who have moved to the USA where life is 'better' but who still long for their roots and find that the life is not better, just the same with different drawbacks. It is a social poem, with a tone of bitterness that is like Larkin's work. From it, one sees Walker's love of his own background.

DAVID WEVILL *1935–*

Wevill was born in Japan in 1935, schooled in Canada (and at Cambridge University), taught in a Burmese university and now lives in the USA: he was a member of The Group (see glossary). His cosmopolitan background is evident in his work.

Self-Portrait at Ten is a Group-like poem and can be compared with Brownjohn's *1939* or, less so, with MacBeth's *The Land-mine*. It captures a moment in time, in which Wevill learnt compassion. *Desperadoes* is structurally a poem like the first, but it is based on a very American kind of subject-matter somehow—the photograph of the dead victims of an outlaw raid. It has pathos and a purposeful anti-climax that focusses thought on the child and her father.

Market Square looks at an American shop window and it is less of a British influenced poem. In technique, it can be seen in the same light as many of the American poems in this book and the moral at the end, written into a visual image, is both obvious and cruel.

Birth of a Shark is a unique poem: there is nothing else like it. A young shark, for the first time, attacks a human bather then discovers the rule of blood by which sharks live by seeing other sharks do what he fails to achieve. Kill. At the end, he lurks like original sin at the base of the sea and this prompts a comparison with Ted Hughes' poetry.

It is strangely fitting that the last poet in the book should be one who draws together in his poetry the threads of so many different poets, their styles, techniques and attitudes – British, American, and Canadian. If a poet is a universal writer, as some would have him (or her) be, then Wevill is a definite poet.

Glossary

alliteration: the repetition of a consonant (sometimes a vowel) sound—eg. slimy snakes slithered softly.

allusion: the referring to another person, object or event usually for comparison or effect; classical allusion, for example, refers to the classical writings of legends.

ambiguity/ambiguous: to have a double meaning/having such a one.

anachronism: a slip (mostly deliberate) of the accuracy of time—to say that Henry VIII drove a car would be an anachronism, for there were no cars in his day.

anti-climax: the act of writing by which excitement or action or impressive ideas are reduced to a lesser state. Also known as *bathos.*

assonance: the repeating of vowel sounds in two syllables without repeating the consonants, making a rhyme—s*ea*m, cr*ea*m/f*i*ght, n*i*ght.

avant garde: a term meaning ahead of current ideas; in other words, the latest, implying experimental or ultra-modern work.

ballad: a word for a simple folk poem which is often a narrative piece, telling a tale. A true ballad consists of four line stanzas with an abcb rhyme scheme, but the ballad form has undergone much change.

bathos: see *anti-climax.*

Beat Poetry/The Beat Poets: The Beat Poets (mainly Ginsberg, Jack Kerouac, Lawrence Ferlinghetti, Gregory Corso and William Burroughs) believed that poetry was alive to modern realities and arose from an oral tradition. They followed a creed of personal freedom, travel, and reacted against the set standards of society as they saw it—the American way of life. Their poetry avoided the rules of verse-making and the restrictions these imposed on style, and it dealt with subjects that poetry had not handled before; it was self-conscious but far-reaching in its appeal. They came to the fore through the San Francisco 'renaissance' of the mid-1950s.

blank verse: any unrhymed verse. It originally had a set metre with lines that were syntactically complete (see *syntax*) and ended in a punctuation mark, each line being self-contained and not 'running on' into the next by way of meaning. Nowadays, it is a looser form altogether and has relaxed the basic rules. Some people now term the looser variety of blank verse as free verse.

cadence: either (a) the modulation or regulation of sound of a word (whether read or spoken) or (b) the rhythm or rhythmical quality of words.

caesura:　a break in a line, usually between words within a metrical foot (see *metre*). It is, in modern blank verse, more widely interpreted as a break in a line or in meaning: some critics regard it as being able to come at (or as) the end of a line when the meaning continues into the next line—eg. in Hall's *The Old Pilot's Death:*
> The glass over the instruments
> has broken, and the red arrows. . . . The caesura would come

after the word 'instruments'.

catharsis:　a cleaning out of emotions, a means by which emotions are understood and appreciated by the act of purging. In a way, to talk over a problem with a friend, setting the problem in perspective, is an act of catharsis. Much confessional poetry is cathartic—by talking about oneself, one understands one's troubles and situation.

chronology/chronological:　the happening of things in order within time, one after another.

cliché:　a phrase that, because it has been used so often, has lost its power or impact—eg. the silvery stream, the golden sunlight.

climax:　the leading up to an event of importance, or the event itself—in Kinnell's *The Bear*, the long trailing of the animal leads up to the climax of finding it and, then, becoming it.

coinage:　the making of new words to suit a particular task—Berryman does this with his invented word *highlone* in *In Memoriam.*

colour imagery:　see *imagery*.

collage:　artistically, it is a picture made up by glued fragments of other pictures or shapes; in poetry, it refers to a form in which many objects are listed, for a final effect—eg. a poem entitled *The Doctor's Surgery* might go
> Syringes, scalpels, surgical cloth;
> the ether smell, the shining steel,
> the stethoscope, the drug ampules,
> the black leather couch—they see pain
> and cure it in this aweful room.

and would be a collage poem. (See *reportage* for a similar technique.)

confessional poet:　one whose work is very personal in its basic subject matter, which looks inward and judges the self and, by doing this, comments upon others and comes to terms with private matters (see also *catharsis*).

consonant/consonance:　a consonant is a letter (other than a vowel) the sound of which is made by stopping or obstructing the breath; consonance is a combination of these sounds in a pleasing, harmonious or meaningful manner—eg. hissing sighs which is sibilant, meaning it uses the 's' sound. The consonance gives the words an additional depth of interpretation.

contrived/contrivance: if a poem is said to be contrived, this implies that it is forced and somehow lacking in artistic truth; the poet has over-planned or designed his work to the detriment of the original idea.

conversational style: see *idiom*.

cosmopolitan: of international standing, interest or appeal.

dialogue: a conversation between two or more people.

diarial: like a diary.

diction: the use of words, basically, or the way in which something is expressed in words.

drama/dramatic: writing with a strong action to it, which often relates it closely to real life or characters; dramatic is the adjective.

eclogue: a short, pastoral poem. See *pastoral poetry*.

elegy: a poem written in memory of someone, usually after their death. An epitaph, if a poem, is an example of an elegy.

emphasis: in speech (or spoken poetry), it is the inflexion or stressing of words to press for a certain meaning—eg. 'I *hate* all apples' which is to say that apples are really horrible to me. It can mean the stressing of ideas that are written down, sometimes implying more than is stated.

enigma/enigmatic: mysterious, puzzling, possibly because little is known or understood about the subject being considered; if a writer is enigmatic, he is usually implied to be secretive, unexpected or out of the ordinary.

esoteric: known only to those who are sharing in the specific knowledge; Ginsberg's poetry is esoteric in that you will get a lot more out of it if you are knowledgeable in Buddhist teachings.

fable: a piece of literature founded on myths or legends; it sometimes carries a lesson or message in it.

free verse: very loosely constructed verse with virtually no basic structure to it. See *blank verse*.

The Group: The Group was a collection of poets who met at regular intervals to criticize each other's work, to compare and contrast their poetry and to follow certain poetic ideals. They had their beginnings in Cambridge in 1952 and moved to London in 1955: they ceased to come together in the mid-1960s, although some of them continued to meet under a new name. The main members were Martin Bell, Alan Brownjohn, George MacBeth, Adrian Mitchell, Peter Redgrove and David Wevill, under the leadership of Philip Hobsbaum and Edward Lucie-Smith (who are not included in this book).

half-rhyme: words that do not fully rhyme (see *rhyme*)—eg. ride/-rode, greet/grate. Assonance and consonance are a variety of half-rhyme, of which there are half a dozen types.

homograph: a word with the same spelling as another word, but with a different meaning.

human condition: a term covering the state of humanity, human existence and human society; it has a very broad base of meaning.

idiom: the form of speech used by everyday people in a certain society, which is peculiar to them—eg. Cockney rhyming slang is the idiom of the East End of London.

imagery: an image is something that represents something else: daffodils are an image of spring-time, for example. Imagery is the use of this technique, of having one thing stand for another. Often, it is easier to give an image, that the reader's (or listener's) mind can expand or know on more than one level, than it is to give a straight factual description; the reader can then give a personal interpretation which allows the poem more scope for emotional reaction. Colour imagery and visual imagery are forms of this technique's application—think of 'the black rocks that sink ships' (black stands for evil) or the 'dead tree like a bloodless set of veins against the sky' (comparison of death, bloodless veins and the tree against a dull background). See also *metaphor, simile* and *symbolism.*

immediacy: directness or having a sense of immediate importance.

impinge: literally, to press something hard; if an idea impinges itself upon one, it strikes one forcibly.

incantation/incantatory: an incantation is a chant or spell-like series of words that seek to do magic or some supernatural action. A prayer is an incantation. Incantatory is the adjective.

internal rhyme: words that rhyme not at the end of a line but within it. It can be that they rhyme with the last word in the line—eg. The fair winds *blew*: the blackbirds *flew* . . . —or with other words within the poem—eg.

> The monks were *fasting* at the dawn,
> And the winds, *blasting* through the trees,
> Tore down huge branches.

irony/ironic: a figure of speech in which what is stated has an opposite meaning—eg. 'What a polite child you have, Mrs. Green', meaning how awful he is, having just eaten the goldfish. Ironic (the adjective) can also mean sardonically, sarcastically or mockingly witty or humorous.

italics: sloping printing often used to emphasize a word—eg. *anthology.*

lament: a poem expressing sorrow.

lyric/lyrical: a short poem having the qualities of music. A lyric usually expresses the personal thoughts of the poet, often on only one topic. Nowadays, lyrical (the adjective) is used to apply to a poem that has a certain aesthetic or artistic beauty to it, especially in its diction and metrical structure.

macabre: gruesome.

metaphor: a figure of speech in which the properties of one object are transferred to another, to further description or the power of the imagery—eg. He is a lion on the rugby field. He doesn't become a large cat when playing rugby; he becomes strong, brave and fearless playing rugby, these being lion-like attributes. (Look at Walker's *Rook Shoot* where the dead birds become 'dark parcels'.)

metre: poetic rhythm which is made from the type and number of groups of syllables to a line. Each group is called a metrical foot and may have two, three or four syllables in it. A line can consist of one to seven feet, each having a certain name—respectively monometer, dimeter, tetrameter, pentameter, hexameter (called an alexandrine) and heptameter. There are twenty-one main types of feet. A detailed explanation of these can be found in critical books on poetic writing and construction (see the book list after this glossary).

moral: a meaning or lesson to be learnt from, often, a fable. It can be applied to other forms—consider the lesson to be learned from Mitchell's *Open Day At Porton.*

The Movement: a group of poets who, in the 1950s, set about to create a new poetic atmosphere after the period of poetry that was written in, and was typical of, the 1940s. They sought to be 'anti-phoney' and worked against the romanticism of the post-war poets, wrote with a sharp attention to technique, irony and syntax. They aimed to write about realism. The main Movement poets are Kingsley Amis (known best as a novelist), Philip Larkin, Elizabeth Jennings and Thom Gunn.

muse: a Muse was one of Zeus' nine goddess daughters who, as beautiful young girls, inspired poetry in men's minds. Nowadays, it is used to mean a source of a poet's inspiration, being regarded as a common, not a proper, noun.

narrative/narrative poem: a narrative is a story and a narrative poem is one that tells a tale.

nostalgia/nostalgic: a feeling of sorrow for something lost or passed by, such as childhood or good times now over. Nostalgic is the adjective.

objective: to be objective is to consider something by standing back from it and looking at it carefully from outside.

onomatopoeia: the marriage of the sound of a word with its sense— eg. Bang! Hush! Thump!

oral poetry: poetry originally written for, or expressed only in, the spoken word.

pastoral poetry: poetry about the countryside, life in it, or the people who inhabit it.

pathetic fallacy: the personification of Mother Nature or the interest of Nature in the activities of men; also the giving to natural objects of human capabilities—eg.

'The skies wept tears
to see the year
turn his old head hoary . . .'

pathos: the feeling in literature which makes the reader sense sadness or pity.

persona/personification: to take on a persona is to take upon oneself the personal qualities of another. Personification is a kind of metaphor where human qualities are given to non-human objects; this interpretation of the word links it to pathetic fallacy.

prolific: to be fertile; in a writer, if he produces a large body of writings then he is said to be prolific.

prose-poem: a poem which entirely, or in parts, adopts the structures of prose (ie non-metrical) language. Not to be confused with free verse which does; at least, if it has no set metrical structure, obey the line or other aspects of verse form.

reportage: the reporting of facts, as in a newspaper; can lack intentional emotive content.

rhyme: corresponding sounds in words, in poetry usually at the end of each line. (See *internal rhyme.*) There are four main types of full rhymes, as opposed to half-rhymes, but their names need not be emphasized.

rhyme scheme: the pattern of the rhyme, best shown by example—consider:

Now is done thy long day's work;
Fold thy palms across thy breast,
Fold thine arms, turn to thy rest.
Let them rave.
Shadows of the silver birk
Sweep the green that folds thy grave.
Let them rave.

the first line is the *a* line, the second *b*; the third line rhymes with the *b* line so becomes also a *b*; the fourth line, not rhyming with any previous, becomes *c* and the fifth line rhymes with *a*, so becomes *a*. And so on. The rhyme scheme then is *abbcacc.*

rhythm: see *metre.*

schematics: the keeping to a scheme or plan.

'school': not an actual school or even a firm group, but just a collection of people who hold to similar ideas or beliefs.

sentimentality: the action of having thoughts that are deeply affected by personal emotion; it is often considered a weakness in modern poetry, because it tends to be regarded as 'sloppy', banal and maudlin.

sestet: see *stanza.*

sibilance: see *consonant.*

simile: a figure of speech whereby one object is compared to another so that each may gain from the other's description—eg. He is like a pig when he eats. He doesn't actually look like a pig, he just eats clumsily, as pigs do. (Not to be confused with metaphor.)

sound poetry: poetry which, regardless of meaning, seeks to work only as music, as a sequence of sounds. (George MacBeth is a leading sound poet in the true sense, with whole poems that are meaningless on the page, but take on qualities of humour when spoken.) An example: Oompa! Oompa! Stickitupyerjumpa!

stanza: a stanza (sometimes called a verse) is a section of a poem, divided from the rest of the poem by a break of one or more line spaces. There are many stanza forms, depending on the number of lines in each. In formal verse, they have set rhyme schemes at times. The most common are couplets (two lines), tercets (3), quatrains (4) and sestets (6): stanzas may, in modern poems, be of any length.

stream of consciousness writing: a technique in which the poet writes down his thoughts and emotions much as they arrive in his head.

style: the manner in which a writer expresses himself. Stylistics are the study of literary style or the application of style by the writer. eg. A simple poetic style would produce:

> All dogs do bark
> When the night is dark.

whereas a more complex style would be:

> But he, unmoved, contemns their idle threat,
>   Secure of fame whene'er he please to fight:
> His cold experience tempers all his heat,
>   And inbred worth doth boasting valour slight.

surrealism: a form of art which, with bizarre imagery, attempts to portray and explain dreams and the subconscious. Surreal or surrealist can also apply to work that goes beyond reality into the recesses of the imagination.

syllable/syllabics: a vocal sound that comes from a single effort which is the building brick of words. Words with one syllable—at, an, a, up; two syllables—before, alone; three syllables— outermost, remotely. And so on. . . . Syllabics is the term for the use of syllables as parts of poetic structure.

symbolism: the use of symbols, which are alike to images, in that they stand for something. Often, they are a little further removed from an exact representation. For example, a man in a white robe with a beard is the visual image we have of Christ, but the cross is the symbol by which we know him.

syntax: the arrangement of words so that they connect to each other to make sense in a sentence. It also refers to the particular constructions of words that an author might use that is special to his style.

technical poet: a loose description of a poet who is skilled at writing verse in strict forms, or very capable in all or many of the forms of poetry writing.

tone: the mood of a poem; the quality of diction and/or syntax; the stressing of syllables; the harmony of ideas with language.

tradition: in the context of this book, the rules or attitudes of poetry that have been handed down from the past.

universal/universality: a poem that is universal can be appreciated or understood very widely. Universality is the ability to be universal in approach.

verse: another name for poetry. Can also mean a stanza (see *stanza*).

visual imagery: imagery that prompts a visual picture in the mind's eye (see *imagery*).

vowel: a sound made by vibrating the vocal chords in the throat or the letter of the alphabet that causes that to happen—*a, e, i, o* and *u.*

Bibliography

The list is arranged alphabetically by author: not all of each author's books are included and it is advised that you seek the help of a librarian or bookseller to find these and others. Titles are given with the names of the publishers in brackets with the date of the book's first publication (except if in paperback, when many issues may have appeared.) Some of the poets' books have not been published in this country but this does not mean that libraries or bookshops cannot get copies of them.

Martin Bell	*Collected Poems: 1937–66* (Macmillan: 1967)
	Penguin Modern Poets 3 (Penguin Books)
John Berryman	all John Berryman's books are published by Faber (London)
Robert Bly	all Robert Bly's books are published by Harper & Row, Inc. in New York (USA); some of his books are published in Britain and his work appears in:
	Penguin Book of American Verse (Penguin Books)
	Contemporary American Poetry (Penguin Books)
	English & American Surrealist Poetry (Penguin Books)
Richard Brautigan	Brautigan's books are published by Simon & Schuster, in New York (USA)
Alan Brownjohn	*A Song of Good Life* (Secker & Warburg: 1975)
Charles Causley	*Collected Poems: 1951–75* (Macmillan: 1975)
Douglas Dunn	*Love or Nothing* (Faber: 1974)
	Barbarians (Faber: 1979)
Allen Ginsberg	all Ginsberg's books are published by City Lights Books of San Francisco: in Britain, his work appears in the same books as Robert Bly's, but not the last, and in
	Penguin Modern Poets 5 (Penguin Books)
Donald Hall	*Kicking the Leaves* (Secker & Warburg: 1979)
Seamus Heaney	his five books are all published by Faber (London) including:
	Field Work (1979), *North* (1975), *Wintering Out* (1972).

William Heyen	William Heyen's books are published by Vanguard in New York (USA); none of his poetry has appeared in book form in Britain
Ted Hughes	all Ted Hughes' books are published by Faber (London) including: *Remains of Elmet* (1979), *Moortown* (1979), *Season Songs* (1976), *Gaudete* (1977), *Cave Birds* (1978)
Galway Kinnell	*The Book of Nightmares* (Omphalos Press: 1978) other books by Kinnell have appeared in Britain, but are no longer on sale; libraries should have them in stock. American editions are published by Houghton, Mifflin Co. in Boston (USA)
Philip Larkin	*The Less Deceived* (Marvell Press: new edition 1977) *The North Ship* (Faber: new edition) *The Whitsun Weddings* (Faber: 1964) *High Windows* (Faber: 1974)
George MacBeth	*Collected Poems: 1958–70* (Macmillan: 1971) *Poems of Love & Death* (Secker & Warburg: 1980) all MacBeth's books are available through public libraries; they may be obtained on request
Adrian Mitchell	*Ride the Nightmare* (Cape: 1971) *The Apeman Cometh* (Cape: 1975)
Brian Patten	*Little Johnny's Confession* (1967), *Notes to the Hurrying Man* (1969), *The Irrelevant Song* (1971), *Vanishing Trick* (1976), *Grave Gossip* (1979): all published by George Allen & Unwin, Ltd
Sylvia Plath	*The Colossus, Ariel, Crossing the Water, Winter Trees:* all in many editions and published by Faber
Peter Redgrove	*Sons of My Skin* (1975), *From Every Chink of the Ark* (1977), *The Weddings at Nether Powers* (1979): all published by Routledge & Kegan Paul
Penelope Shuttle	*The Orchard Upstairs* (Oxford Univ. Press: 1980)
Alan Sillitoe	*Snow on the North Side of Lucifer* (W. H. Allen: 1980)
Robin Skelton	*The Dark Window* (Oxford Univ. Press: 1962) *The Hunting Dark* (Deutsch: 1971) *Timelight* (Heinemann: 1974)

Ken Smith	*Work, Distances* (Swallow Press, Chicago, USA: 1972) *The Pity* (Cape: 1967) *Tristan Crazy* (Bloodaxe Books: 1979)
Stevie Smith	*Two in One* (Longman: 1971)
William Stafford	*Stories That Could Be True* (Harper & Row: New York USA: 1977) Stafford's work also appears in *Contemporary American Poetry* (Penguin Books)
R. S. Thomas	*Selected Poems: 1946–68* (Hart-Davis, McGibbon: 1973) *Frequencies* (Macmillan: 1978)
David Wagoner	*Riverbed; Who Shall be The Sun?* (both books Indiana Univ. Press: London-American Univ. Publishing Group: 1972 & 78 respectively)
Ted Walker	*Fox on a Barn Door* (1965), *The Solitaries* (1967), *The Night Bathers* (1970), *Gloves to the Hangman* (1973), *Burning the Ivy* (1978): all published by Jonathan Cape, Ltd
David Wevill	*Birth of a Shark* (1964), *A Christ of the Ice-Floes* (1966), *Firebreak* (1971), *Where the Arrow Falls* (1973): all published by Macmillan, Ltd

Other books of interest or use:

British Poetry Since 1960   ed. Schmidt & Lindop   (Carcanet Press: 1972)
Considering Poetry   ed. Phythian   (EUP: 1970)
An Introduction to 50 Modern British Poets   ed. Schmidt   (Pan: 1979)
The Modern Poet   ed. Hamilton   (Macdonald: 1968)
Poetry in Crosslight   ed. Thomas   (Longman: 1975)
Poetry in the Making   Ted Hughes   (Faber: 1967)
The Poet's Calling   Robin Skelton   (Heinemann: 1975)
The Practice of Poetry   Robin Skelton   (Heinemann: 1971)
A Theory of Communication   Philip Hobsbaum   (Macmillan: 1970)
Twentieth Century English Poetry   A. Thwaite   (Heinemann: 1978)
A Vision of Reality   Frederick Grubb   (Chatto & Windus: 1965)
Unassigned Frequencies   L. Lieberman   (Univ. of Illinois Press/ American Univ. Publishing Group, London: 1977)

There are *many* record albums of poetry and poets reading their own work available. The following are but a few that are of importance and interest:

Brian Patten reading his poetry   Caedmon TC1300
The Sly Cormorant: Brian Patten   Argo ZSW 607

The Poet Speaks: incl. MacBeth, Mitchell & Wevill   Argo PLP 1086
The Poet Speaks: incl. Redgrove   Argo PLP 1084
The Poet Speaks: incl. Hughes and Plath   Argo PLP 1085
The Poet Speaks: incl. Larkin, Causley & Ken Smith   Argo
    PLP 1088
Poetry 1900–1965: incl. Hughes & Stevie Smith   Longmans 34155
The Poetry & Voice of Ted Hughes   Caedmon TC1535
The Whitsun Weddings: Philip Larkin   Marvell Press LPV6
Peter Redgrove & Peter Porter   Argo PLP 1204
Stevie (soundtrack of the film on her life) CBS 70165

Acknowledgements

Martin Bell: From *Collected Poems 1937–66* (Macmillan). Reprinted by permission of The Martin Bell Literary Estate. **John Berryman:** 'An Afternoon Visit' and 'Canal Smell' both from *Henry's Fate and other poems*; 'In Memoriam' from *Delusions*. Reprinted by permission of Faber & Faber Ltd. **Robert Bly:** 'Counting small-boned bodies' copyright © 1967 by Robert Bly, and 'Sleet Storm on the Merritt Parkway' copyright © 1962 by Robert Bly, both from *Light Around the Body*; 'The Dead Seal near McClure's Beach' from *The Morning Glory* copyright © 1975 by Robert Bly; 'Coming in for Supper' from *This Body is Made of Camphor and Gopherwood* copyright © 1977 by Robert Bly. All reprinted by permission of Harper & Row Publishers, Inc. **Richard Brautigan:** 'The Chinese Checker Players' and 'The Horse That Had a Flat Tire' both from *The Pill Versus the Springhill Mine Disaster*, © 1968 Richard Brautigan (Dell Publ.); 'On the Elevator Going Down' from *June 30: June 30* (Dell Publ.). **Alan Brownjohn:** '1939' and 'Office Party' from *The Lions Mouth*; 'A 202' from *Sandgrains On a Tray*. Reprinted by permission of Macmillan, London and Basingstoke. **Charles Causley:** From *Collected Poems 1951–1975* (Macmillan 1975). Reprinted by permission of David Highman Associates Ltd. **Douglas Dunn:** 'Young Women in Rollers' from *Terry Street* (1969); 'The Wealth' from *Barbarians* (1979). Reprinted by permission of Faber & Faber Ltd. **Allen Ginsberg:** From Mind Breaths: *Poems Nineteen Seventy-two to Nineteen Seventy-seven* (City Lights, 1978). **Donald Hall:** 'An Airstrip in Essex 1960'; 'The Old Pilot's Death' and 'The Farm', all from *A Roof of Tiger Lilies* (Deutsch). Reprinted by permission of the author. 'Maple Syrup' from *Kicking the Leaves* copyright © 1976 by Donald Hall. Reprinted by permission of Harper & Row, Publishers, Inc. **Seamus Heaney:** 'The Grauballe Man' and 'Orange Drums, Tyrone 1966' both from *North* (1975); 'The Outlaw' from *Door into the Dark* (1969); 'Follower' from *Death of a Naturalist* (1969); 'A New Song' from *Wintering Out* (1972). All reprinted by permission of Faber & Faber Ltd. **William Heyen:** 'Driving at Dawn' from *Depth of Field* (Baton Rouge: Louisiana State Univ. Press, 1970), © 1970 William Heyen; 'Spring', © William Heyen. 'Mantle' first appeared in *Poetry*, © 1979 William Heyen. All used by permission of the author. 'Legend of the Tree at the Center of the World', 'Son Dream', 'Pet's Death' and 'Worming at Short Beach' all from *Long Island Light: Poems & a Memoir*, © 1979 William Heyen. Reprinted by permission of Vanguard Press, Inc. **Ted Hughes:** 'A Bedtime Story' from *Crow* (1972); 'Wodwo' from *Wodwo* (1967); 'The Burrow Wolf' from *Earth Owl and Other Moon People* (1963); 'A Motorbike' and 'Tractor' both from *Moortown* (1979); 'Cock-crows' from *Remains of Elmert* (1979). All reprinted by permission of Faber & Faber Ltd. 'A Solstice' from *All Around the Year*, edited by Michael Morpurgo and published by John Murray. Reprinted by permission of Faber & Faber Ltd. **Galway Kinnell:** 'The River that is East' and 'Spindrift' both from *Poems of the Night*; 'The Bear' from

Acknowledgements

Body Rags. Reprinted by permission of Rapp and Whiting Ltd. **Philip Larkin:** 'Mr Bleaney' from *The Whitsun Weddings* (1964); 'Going, Going' and 'The Explosion' both from *High Windows* (1974). All reprinted by permission of Faber & Faber Ltd. **George MacBeth:** 'Death of a Ferrari' and 'A Poem for Breathing' both from *Poems of Love & Death* (Secker & Warburg); 'The Land-Mine' from *The Colour of Blood* (Macmillan); 'Marshall' from *The Night of Stones* (Macmillan). All reprinted by permission of the author. **Adrian Mitchell:** 'Open Day at Porton' and 'Old Age Report' from *Ride the Night-Mare* (1971); 'Lady Macbeth in the Saloon Bar Afterwards' and 'Dumb Insolence' both from *The Apeman Cometh* (1975). All reprinted by permission of the author and Jonathan Cape Ltd. **Brian Patten:** 'A Blade of Grass' from *Vanishing Trick* (1976); 'Albatross Ramble' from *Irrelevant Song* (1971); 'Old Crock' from *Notes to the Hurrying Man* (1969); 'Little Johnny's Final Letter' from *Little Johnny's Confession* (1967). All reprinted by permission of George Allen & Unwin. **Sylvia Plath:** 'The Arrival of the Bee Box' from *Ariel* (Faber), © Ted Hughes 1965; 'Pheasant' from *Crossing the Water* (Faber), © Ted Hughes 1971; 'All the Dead Dears' from *The Colossus* (Faber), © Ted Hughes 1976; 'Rabbit Catcher' from *Winter Trees* (Faber), © Ted Hughes 1971; 'The Goring' from *Crystal Gazer* (Rainbow Press) and 'Old Ladies Home' from *Lyonesse* (Rainbow Press) both collections © Ted Hughes 1971. All reprinted by permission of Olwyn Hughes, Literary Agent. **Peter Redgrove:** 'Thirteen Ways of Looking at a Blackboard' and 'A Storm' both from *The Collector and Other Poems* (1959); 'Design' from *The Force and Other Poems* (1966); 'At the Edge of the Wood' and 'Gentlemen' both from *The Nature of Cold Weather and Other Poems* (1961); 'Who's Your Daddy?' from *From Every Chink of the Ark* (1977). All reprinted by permission of Routledge & Kegan Paul Ltd. **Penelope Shuttle:** From *Autumn Piano* (Rondo Publications 1974). Reprinted by permission of the author. 'Granite Valentine' first appeared in Samphire Magazine, 1974. **Alan Sillitoe:** From *Snow on the North Face of Lucifer* (1980). Reprinted by permission of W. H. Allen & Co. Ltd. **Robin Skelton:** 'John Arthur' and 'Ballad of Billy Barker' both from *Selected Poems* (McClelland & Stewart, 1968); 'The Friday Fish' from *The Hunting Dark* (Deutsch 1971). Reprinted by permission of the author. **Ken Smith:** 'The Pity', 'The Hunter' and 'Spring Poem' all from *The Pity* (Cape 1967). Reprinted by permission of the author. 'A description of the Lichway . . .' from *Working Distances* (Swallow Press 1972). Reprinted by permission of the author and Ohio University Press. **Stevie Smith:** From *The Collected poems of Stevie Smith* (Allen Lane 1975). Reprinted by permission of James MacGibbon, Executor. **William Stafford:** 'Traveling through the Dark', copyright © 1960 by William Stafford; 'Montana Eclogue', © 1966 by William Stafford, originally appeared in *The New Yorker*; 'Ice-Fishing', © 1960 by William Stafford, and 'In the Old Days', © 1967 by William Stafford, all from *Stories That Could be True* (1977). Reprinted by permission of Harper & Row, Publishers, Inc. 'They Say' from *Two About Music*. Reprinted by permission of the author. **R. S. Thomas:** From *Selected Poems: 1946–68* (Hart-Davis 1973). Reprinted by permission of Granada Publishing Ltd. **David Wagoner:** From *Riverbed*, © 1972 by Indiana University Press. Reprinted by permission of the publisher. **Ted Walker:** 'Three Boy's' from *The Night Bathers* (1970); 'Rook Shoot' and 'Easter Poem' from *Fox on a Barn Door* (1965); 'The Emigres' from *Gloves to the Hangman* (1973). All reprinted by permission of the author and Jonathan Cape Ltd. **David Wevill:** 'Self-portrait at Ten' from *A Christ of the Ice-Floes* (1966); 'Desperadoes' and 'The Birth of a Shark' from *Birth of a Shark* (1964); 'Market Square' from *Firebreak* (1971). All reprinted by permission of Macmillan, London and Basingstoke.

Every effort has been made to trace and contact copyright owners. If there are any omissions the publishers will be happy to give the full acknowledgements at the first reprint.

Index